Grave-robbers & Bodysnatchers

IN DEVON

I am indebted to
Paul A C Richards
for researching the archives
in Tasmania

"I need bodies and I want them fresh"

Grave-robbers & Bodysnatchers
IN DEVON

Patricia Gray

HALSGROVE

First published in Great Britain by Halsgrove, 2009

British Library Cataloguing-in-Publication Data
A CIP record for this title is available from the British Library

ISBN 978 1 84114 855 7

HALSGROVE
Halsgrove House,
Ryelands Industrial Estate,
Bagley Road, Wellington, Somerset TA21 9PZ
Tel: 01823 653777   Fax: 01823 216796
email: sales@halsgrove.com

Part of the halsgrove group of companies
Information on all Halsgrove titles is available at: www.halsgrove.com

Printed and bound by Short Run Press, Exeter

Contents

1 Thomas Vaughan 6

2 A Highly-Paid Low-Risk Job 9

3 The Holywell Mount Affair 18

4 Escape to the Country 21

5 The Master Fiend 29

6 Murder for Money 36

7 Not Guilty 40

8 Unholy Affairs 45

9 Murder 52

10 For The Last Time 66

11 The Trial 73

12 The Mystery 84

13 Aftermath at Stoke Damerel 87

14 Transportation 92

15 The Misery of the Voyages 99

16 Servitude in Van Diemen's Land 103

17 The Italian Boy 117

18 The Demise of Grave-robbing 124

   Bibliography 127

CHAPTER ONE

Thomas Vaughan

Thomas Vaughan was born in Limerick, Ireland, but met his downfall in Devon. He had inflicted distress on a great many people before he broke his own long-held rules and came to grief in Devonport. Brought up in the Roman Catholic faith, he was undone in a Protestant burial ground.

Patrick Vaughan and his wife had four daughters before their son, Thomas, was born in 1790. At some time Thomas came to London where he became well-known to the officers at the Union Hall Magistrates' Court which dealt with petty criminals operating in a large part of South London. He may have learned of the fortune to be made supplying the newly-dead to the anatomy schools of London while he was working as a stonemason's labourer repairing church buildings or erecting headstones in graveyards. Grave-robbing was a very unpleasant business dealing in putrefying corpses but it paid well. For thirteen years Thomas Vaughan supplied the surgeons and anatomy schools with "subjects" or "things". He obtained them by all the practices used by bodysnatchers from robbing the graves of the newly-dead to using a female accomplice to acquire them from workhouses. He was audacious, and on one occasion he broke into the mortuary of a London hospital, stole two bodies and sold them to the mortuary of another London hospital. He was among the ten men named as the top bodysnatchers. He was the only one of them to end up in Van Diemen's Land.

Thomas Vaughan regularly supplied bodies to Sir Astley Cooper, the most eminent surgeon of his day. He was made a baronet in 1821 for

Astley Cooper was born the son of a Norfolk clergyman. His uncle was William Cooper, appointed as a staff surgeon at St Thomas' and Guy's Hospital and it was there that he started his medical studies. He was also taught by John Hunter and in the winter of 1787 he also visited the anatomy department at the University of Edinburgh. In 1789 he was appointed demonstrator in anatomy at St Thomas' and in 1783 he gave lectures in anatomy for the Company of Surgeons. In 1800 he joined Guy's Hospital. He has been regarded by many as a leading surgeon of his day making numerous academic contributions to surgery and anatomy.

removing a cyst from the head of King George IV. Sir Astley's biographer, his nephew Bransby Cooper, described Thomas Vaughan as a man of "bad character, without common prudence and of dissolute and drunken habits". Sir Astley told a Parliamentary Select Committee that the men who supplied him were "the lowest dregs of degradation". He must nonetheless have had some trust in them for he also told the Select Committee that his men could obtain for him the body of anyone he wanted from anywhere in the kingdom. In 1820 a former patient of the surgeon died at Beccles in Suffolk.

"The Reward of Cruelty" is one of William Hogarth's most famous and clearly unforgettable engravings. Convicted and executed, Tom Nero's body has been delivered to the Royal College of Surgeons for an anatomy lesson.

7

Knowing Mr Cooper's continued interest in the case, the attending doctor informed him of the death. The surgeon was keen to know how the ligatured aneurysmal blood vessels had fared in the body in the years since the operation had been performed. He wanted to see if he could learn anything which would help him improve procedure if he needed to do another such operation and he wanted to obtain the body part for his personal museum. He asked his intermediary to make arrangements for Thomas Vaughan and William Hollis to obtain the body "cost what it may". Vaughan and Hollis obtained the body, though how they did it was not revealed, and their expenses appear in Sir Astley's account book:

Coach for two there and back	£3.12s.0d
Guards and coachmen	£0. 6s.0d
Expenses for two days	£1.14s.6d
Carriage for subject, and porter	£0.12s.6d
Subject	£7. 7s.0d
	£13. 12s.0d

Sir Astley had a museum of examples of various human conditions he had come across in his career as a surgeon, and no doubt he added the specimen from Beccles to his collection.

CHAPTER TWO

A Highly-Paid, Low-Risk Job

Doctors always want to improve the treatment they give their patients. To do this they have to know the structure of the human body and how it works. To gain that knowledge they have to be able to cut up and examine corpses. Throughout history it had been a problem for the medical profession where to find bodies which they could dissect. The earliest surviving written documents detailing the fascination that man has always had for the interior of his body are clay tablets from around 4000 BC. The cuneiform script impressed upon the tablets can be translated, some of it giving excellent descriptions of the insides of men.

Doctors were discouraged from surgery by the edict from the Council of Tours in 1163 whereby the church abhorred the spilling of blood. It was, therefore, often barbers who performed bloodletting, tooth drawing and, later, midwifery. Surgeons throughout history have had a long association with barbers, because medical men denied them professional status. Today this is recognised in the title given to consultant surgeons, who are always addressed as "Mister".

When the Barbers' Company and the Surgeons' Company united by royal charter in 1540 King Henry VIII awarded them the bodies of four hanged felons annually for dissection. King Charles II increased the number to six. In 1745 the surgeons formed their own Company of Surgeons which in 1800 became the Royal College of Surgeons, the body which granted them qualification.

In 1752 Parliament passed an Act which was intended to deter the crime of murder. It said that when a murderer had been tried, convicted and hanged, the body was not to be buried but either hung in chains from a gibbet or given to the surgeons to advance knowledge of anatomy. When a criminal sentenced to dissection had been hanged, before the large crowd which always gathered on such occasions, the corpse was handed by the hangman to the surgeons waiting below the gallows. The body would be cut open, dissected and studied before the remains were put on public exhibition. Often the family or friends of the hanged person would try to seize the body before the surgeons could receive it. Sometimes they were then able to revive the body if the hanging had not succeeded in killing the condemned. Even surgeons sometimes found themselves reviving victims of a hangman's incompetence. Sometimes families tried to bribe officials to keep the corpse from the surgeons. It was not uncommon for surgeons to employ agents to bargain with prisoners condemned to hanging (but not to dissection) offering to pay expenses or to provide for their family following hanging in return for the body being handed over to the surgeons. At a time when most people believed they would arrive in Heaven looking much the same as they had while on Earth, the thought that they were going to end up as a pile of bits and pieces, thus ruining their chance of resurrection, was greatly to be feared.

William Hunter had trained as a surgeon in Paris where there was a plentiful supply of unclaimed dead paupers from the hospitals and mortuaries. Each student had his own corpse to dissect. When Hunter opened a private anatomy school in London he taught in what was called "the Parisian manner", that is to say each student had a body to dissect.

The advantage to students of doing dissection themselves as opposed to merely watching it being demonstrated caused competition between Hunter's school and the other hospital and private schools and led to an increased demand for bodies. All medical students had to pay for their tuition so there was financial pressure on the schools in the competition for students. The schools functioned only in the winter time when decomposition of bodies was slower than in summer. By the beginning of the

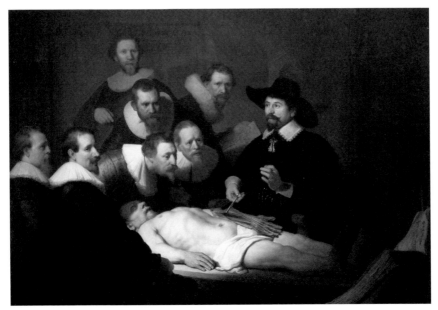

The Anatomy Lesson of Dr Nicolaes Tulp is a 1632 oil painting by Rembrandt. Dr Tulp is pictured explaining the musculature of the arm to medical professionals. The corpse is that of the criminal Aris Kindt, strangled earlier that day for armed robbery. Some of the spectators are various patrons who paid commissions to be included in the painting. The event can be dated to 16 January 1632: the Amsterdam Guild of Surgeons, of which Tulp was official City Anatomist, permitted only one public dissection a year, and the body would have to be that of an executed criminal.

nineteenth century there were very many more medical students than there were hanged criminals. The number of offences which carried the death penalty had been decreasing over the years while the number of medical schools had increased. Between 1805 and 1820 there was a yearly average of eighty executions in England and Wales, an inadequate number to meet the annual needs of approximately one thousand anatomy students. Although the supply was supplemented illegally by bodies provided from prisons and hospitals by the authorities, the total was still inadequate. It was considered that over the course of his medical education each student needed three bodies; two to dissect and one on which to practice operating. Surgeons and anatomists became so desperate for bodies they could use to demonstrate dissection and teach anatomy that they began digging up the newly-dead themselves until the Edinburgh College of Surgeons forbade the practice, and in 1721 the indentures for apprentice surgeons included a clause binding them not to become involved in exhumation.

So the surgeons turned to petty criminals to do the exhumation for them and grave-robbing came to be a highly paid, low-risk job. Many years later, in evidence to a Select Committee set up by Parliament to enquire into the manner of obtaining and dissecting bodies, it was said that a bodysnatcher could make a good living "if he is a sober man, acts with judgement and supplies the schools". Schools paid promptly, treated suppliers well, and never enquired the source of the "subject" as corpses were called. Poor judgement and supplying other outlets such as individual surgeons, physicians, artists, sculptors or students could lead to downfall. Bodysnatchers, grave-robbers, "sack-em-up men" or resurrectionists were the interchangeable names given to the many petty criminals who took part in the trade. Drink was a major preoccupation with some resurrectionists. The most successful ones remained sober and invested their considerable profits in property. Thomas Vaughan was one of about ten practitioners who were the "top men" among grave-robbers. Grave-robbing was a relatively safe occupation but those involved had much to fear from discovery by the public.

According to the law a dead body did not belong to anyone and was said to have no cash value, so the law did not treat the theft of a body in the same way it treated theft of property. Grave-robbing was not a crime it was a misdemeanour and as such carried only light punishments. Taking something off the body such as clothes, shroud or jewellery was classed as theft and punishments for it were harsh. Most bodysnatchers were very aware of the difference in the punishments and made it a practice to steal only the body although there were exceptions where grave-clothes were stolen and sold as "second-hand". Thomas Vaughan robbed graves for thirteen years before he made the mistake of taking more than the body.

A skilled man working in a town might earn as much as thirty shillings a week. Surgeons paid between forty-two shillings and £14 for a body and a man could raise several in a night. In 1828 the average price for a body was eight guineas. Male bodies were preferred to female and children's bodies brought in less money than adults. Children's bodies were graded as "big smalls", "smalls" or foetuses. Jewish bodies were highly prized because Jewish people bury soon after death so those bodies were less decomposed when they reached the schools.

Not only did surgeons pay well but if a regular supplier, like Thomas Vaughan, got in trouble with the law, the surgeons paid for lawyers to defend him in Court. If a regular supplier needed cash to put up as a surety so that he could get bail, then the surgeons supplied the money. If a regular bodysnatcher found himself in prison the surgeons supplied a sum of money each week so that the man could buy himself a less uncomfortable stay and, of course, during such a man's incarceration the surgeons supported the man's family if he had one. Some grave-robbers were paid "finishing money" which was a bonus based on the services performed for their surgeon employer, such as the number of bodies and/or the quality. On 10 May 1821, for instance, Sir Astley Cooper paid Vaughan and Hollis "finishing money" of £6.6s. each.

The demand for "subjects" was so great there was an import trade bringing them into this country from Ireland and the Continent. Dublin became the hub of the illegal export trade with Le Havre, France, close behind. There are tales of ships' captains investigating stinking cargoes, of sticking exploratory hands into barrels and finding putrid flesh.

In spite of the law's contention that a dead body had no cash value, corpses were in fact changing hands for money. Dishonest undertakers were known to bury coffins filled with sand after they had sold the body to the resurrectionists. Bodies were often kept at the deceased's home between death and burial and many a time a body was stolen almost from under the noses of the mourners. Bodies were stolen from Coroners' premises and undertakers' premises. Thomas Vaughan stole two bodies from the mortuary of one London hospital and sold them to the mortuary of another London hospital. Sometimes sextons were in league with the bodysnatchers. They might remove the body and bury an empty or a sand-filled coffin. Some simply removed the body from the coffin when they were left, to refill the grave with earth and then put the body a few inches below the soil so that the grave-robber could find it easily. William Hollis, another of the "top" bodysnatchers and a man who worked closely with Thomas Vaughan, had been a sexton but lost his job when it was discovered he was assisting grave-robbers. Bransby Cooper said Hollis was "one of the greatest villains ever connected to this or any other calling". Hollis later had a hackney carriage business but ended up destitute. A rector of Stockport was allegedly in league with grave-robbers to take the bodies of the poor from his churchyard and convey them to his brother-in-law, a surgeon. According to the January 1829 issue of the *Lancet* one graveyard owned by an anatomist charged for burying the body which he then dug up and sold to his pupils. The London teaching hospitals left large baskets on their forecourts which bodysnatchers could borrow to collect and deliver subjects.

The resurrectionists kept a watchful eye on workhouses and infirmaries. When they learned that someone was dead or dying, a female associate would go to the pauper's bedside, pretend to be a grieving relative and try to claim the body, supposedly for burial. If successful, the body was sold to the surgeons. Parish authorities were only too pleased to be free of the cost of a burial.

In the minute book of the parish of St Thomas, Bermondsey, London, is a record of a meeting held in 1795 "to discover the predations in Lambeth Burial Ground" which states that in addition to bodies and body parts being taken for surgeons, a man called the Articulator was buying corpses during the winter half of the year, and making them into skeletons which were sold not only in all parts of the Kingdom but also sold in America and the West Indies. The minutes recorded that "set prices for bodies were two guineas and a crown for adults, and for everyone under

Tyburn was one of London's principal sites of execution. In 1571, the "Tyburn Tree" was erected near the modern Marble Arch. The "Tree" or "Triple Tree" was a novel form of gallows, comprising a horizontal wooden triangle supported by three legs (an arrangement known as a "three legged mare" or "three legged stool"). Several felons could thus be hanged at once, and so the gallows was occasionally used for mass executions, such as that on 23 June 649 when 24 prisoners, 23 men and one woman, were hanged simultaneously, having been conveyed there in eight carts. After executions, the bodies would be buried nearby or in later times removed for dissection by anatomists.

age six shillings for the first foot and nine per inch for all it measures more in length". The representatives of the various London parishes at that meeting decided to try to get a Bill passed through Parliament to make stealing bodies a capital offence. They did not succeed.

Some of the body-snatchers went to Spain and preyed on the dead of the Peninsular War. Most of the bodies supplied to the surgeons were those of poor people. The rich could, and did, protect their dead from theft by using metal coffins, or putting the body in triple coffins, vaults or mortsafes. A mortsafe was a cage of iron bars sunk into the soil around the coffin or fixed in concrete above the grave or simply put around the grave site to protect it. Some people delayed burial until the body was too decomposed to attract the bodysnatchers. The well-to-do could afford to have graves dug very deep or to have the burial take place in a remote country graveyard. Rich people could afford to pay servants to stand guard over a body although it was not unknown for servants to "guard" an empty coffin after they had sold the corpse. Poor people were likely to be unable to afford a private burial and had to rely on the parish for a pauper's funeral. Often the parish would dig a large deep square pit or trench into which the flimsy coffins used for the poor were put but the pits were left open perhaps for weeks and not backfilled until they were full, which left the grave-robbers with easy access to a guaranteed supply. Even when the pit was filled-in often the soil was only a few inches deep on top of the coffins.

Mortsafes at a churchyard in Logierait, Perth and Kinross, Scotland. The mortsafe was invented in about 1816. These were iron or iron-and-stone devices of great weight, in many different designs. Often they were complex heavy iron contraptions of rods and plates, padlocked together; examples have been found close to all Scottish medical schools. A plate was placed over the coffin and rods with heads were pushed through holes in it. These rods were kept in place by locking a second plate over the first to form extremely heavy protection. It would be removed by two people with keys. They were placed over the coffins for about six weeks, then removed for further use when the body inside was sufficiently decayed. There is a model of a mortsafe of this type in Aberdeen Museum. Sometimes a church bought them and hired them out. Societies were also formed to purchase them and control their use, with annual membership fees, and charges made to non-members.

The only way the poor could protect their dead was to mix sticks and straw with the earth over the coffin to make it difficult for wooden spades. It was the vulnerability of the graves of the poor which led to the custom of the poor paying tiny weekly sums to insurance companies to ensure there would be the money for a "decent burial". It was said that the poor were prepared to pay death insurance before life insurance.

The tools of the bodysnatcher's trade were a wooden shovel, which made less noise than a metal one, a "dark lanthorn" which was a lantern which let out only a narrow beam of light to shine where necessary, ropes and some hooks. Bodysnatchers worked in small groups. One man would keep lookout while a hole was dug at the head of the grave down to the coffin. To have removed all the earth with which the grave had been filled would have taken time and increased the chance of the grave-robbers being detected so only about one-third of the coffin would be exposed. Hooks attached to ropes were put under the lid, while the earth on the rest of the coffin acted as a counterweight, and the lid was ripped open. The body was drawn out of the coffin with ropes, stripped and the grave clothes tossed back into the grave before it was back-filled. A grave-robber could steal from a burial ground for as long a time as no one realised the graves were being interfered with. Thomas Vaughan was a very careful worker. He laid canvas sheets either side of the new grave and the earth was dug out on to the canvas sheets so that when he had backfilled the hole he would shake the canvas sheets on top of the earth leaving the site looking untouched. Some grave-robbers, like Thomas Vaughan, had a horse and cart with which to transport themselves, tools and bodies.

CHAPTER THREE

The Holywell Mount Affair

The most successful of all the bodysnatchers was a man called Murphy. He was tall, stout and with a broad, flat, open face. Although uneducated, he was a very shrewd and clever man. He was so industrious that Cooper records that "on one occasion he was paid at one school £72 for six subjects and then the same evening at another school received £72 for another six subjects. Out of this Murphy would have had to pay four or five underlings in his employ but not at a higher rate than £5 each, leaving Murphy with a splendid profit".

Once when Murphy was walking past a non-conformist chapel, he realised it contained a burial vault. He approached the minister with a story about selecting a burial place for his wife and was allowed down into the vault where he slid back the bolts so that he could re-enter later. That night he returned and removed the teeth from the corpses. He later sold them for £60. All teeth fixed in dentures in those days came from the dead and supplying dentists was a lucrative sideline for grave-robbers. Not surprisingly Murphy accumulated a fortune which he invested in property. To own house property was the goal of all the leaders of the grave-robbing gangs. When Murphy retired he became a respectable property owner.

Vaughan came to suspect that Murphy had a secret source of bodies. Perhaps Murphy bought more property than his overt doings would finance. There was already rivalry between Vaughan and Murphy who both supplied "subjects" to Sir Astley Cooper. Vaughan made it his business to try and discover Murphy's secret. He found that Murphy, and another bodysnatcher called Patrick Connolly, had long had an arrangement with a Mr Whackett, the sexton/grave-digger of a private burial ground at Holywell Mount, Shoreditch London. The ground was owned by two elderly ladies who lived in a house which fronted the burial ground and, unbeknown to them, their employee, Whackett, was selling the bodies buried there to Murphy and Connolly. Bransby Cooper says the arrangement operated from 1810 to 1820.

Vaughan with one of his colleagues, William Hollis, made it his business to meet Whackett. Vaughan tried to deceive Whackett into believing that he was in partnership with Murphy and thus entitled to a share in the plentiful supply in the burial ground. In spite of all Vaughan's efforts to charm Whackett refused. Totally enraged by Vaughan's persistence, Whackett crossed the road and entered a public house full of labourers drinking. He called out to them and pointing through the window at Vaughan and Hollis told them that "those men have been trying to bribe me to allow them to plunder my burial ground". Everyone there hated bodysnatchers and rushed out of the pub intent on capturing Vaughan and Hollis and delivering instant justice to the villains. When the bodysnatchers saw the crowd they realised their situation and had already started running. They got away but, their scheme frustrated, ran into the nearest Police Court.

They found a magistrate was sitting and the Court was crowded with people. Vaughan shouted out in a very loud voice that if the magistrate sent police officers to Holywell Mount burial ground they would find all the graves were empty because the gravedigger, Whackett, had sold the dead to bodysnatchers. The public feared and abhorred grave-robbing so as one man the Court emptied and the crowd set off for Holywell Mount. The numbers swelled as they made their way to the burial ground.

They broke down the gates and began digging open the graves. Whackett was captured and made to watch. As more and more graves proved to be empty the anger of the crowd increased. Whackett was thrown into the bottom of one of the deepest of the empty graves and the crowd began backfilling it, shovelling earth on top of Whackett. He was only saved from death by the arrival of the police who had followed the crowd from the Police Court.

Frustrated, the crowd turned to Whackett's house where they seized his wife and children whom they dragged through a nearby stagnant pond and then went back to destroy every bit of the family's furniture and furnishings. They worked out the last of their anger by breaking all the windows in the house of the two elderly ladies who owned the burial ground but who were totally unaware of Whackett's dealings.

When the news reached Murphy that he had lost a plentiful and easy supply of merchandise he determined to have his revenge on Vaughan and Hollis at the earliest opportunity.

CHAPTER FOUR

Escape to the Country

Vaughan and Hollis appreciated the likely consequence of what they had done and thought it prudent to give Murphy time to cool down, so they left the capital and went to Kent. They robbed the graveyards in that county and sent the bodies back to the London anatomy schools until the day when the Customs and Excise decided to take action against smugglers operating in Kent.

On 1 November 1821, a Mr R Willard, a Customs and Excise officer, was on the lookout for contraband goods near Foots Cray in Kent. He stopped a horse-drawn cart and, upon searching it, found it to contain five dead bodies; two men, two women and a child, concealed in sacks. All except one appeared to have been recently interred. The instant the cart was stopped, the two men driving it jumped out and made off in different directions. They were not pursued. Upon enquiry it was found that all five bodies had been stolen from Maidstone; three from the churchyard and the other two from the adjoining new burial ground. After being robbed of their contents the coffins had been thrown into the graves again and covered with earth. The local officials sent the bodies back to Maidstone to be re-interred in their original graves.

The cart had on it a board with a fictitious name and place and, two men having often been seen going up and down the road, it was realised that grave-robbing had been carried on in that area for some time.

Vaughan fled Kent and moved his activities to Berkshire. By the time the Maidstone police caught up with him he was in Reading gaol serving a sentence of three months' imprisonment for stealing a body from the churchyard at Bray, Berkshire (the church associated with the traditional song about the turncoat "Vicar of Bray"). As soon as he had completed his sentence and been released he was arrested by the Maidstone police.

Although when Vaughan had lived and worked in Kent he had used the alias "Thomas Smith" his real name was known to the authorities. On 4 June 1822 he appeared in Court in Maidstone charged, in his own name, with being concerned with two others in stealing five bodies from Maidstone churchyard. There were two bills of indictment. In one the charge said that he "...with force and arms unlawfully, voluntarily and indecently did dig open the grave and carry away the body of Mary Bacon to the great indecency of christian burial to the evil example of all others...". It was said that he had been engaged in grave-robbing for the last five years. He was remanded in custody.

He reappeared in Court on 24 June when depositions were taken from the sexton, the Foots Cray Customs and Excise officer, and a waggoner from Farningham who gave evidence that he had seen the cart go up and down the road and had particularly noticed Vaughan on it, as he had seen him previously in custody at Sevenoaks on a similar charge. Vaughan was committed for trial at the Quarter Sessions. By binding himself in a bond of £100 to appear at the trial and by obtaining two other sureties of £50 each, he obtained bail. When due to attend Court again in October he was absent. One of the sureties told the Court that Vaughan was prevented from attending due to an illness occasioned by the loss of blood, but the Court refused to accept the excuse and ordered Vaughan's £100 to be forfeited.

The following item in the *Brighton Chronicle* of 3 December 1822 gives rise to speculation that, when released on bail in June, Vaughan might have gone from Kent to Sussex:-

Died at Brighton, a few days since, the wife of a labouring man and the funeral had the appearance of all the solemnity usual on such melancholy occasions. Soon after the ceremony was supposed to be over, a neighbour waited to console with him on the severe loss he had sustained, who, after a short conversation observed the coffin was still in the house but the wrong way up, which lead to the enquiry, where his wife was? After some hesitation the man replied when first he had his wife he bought her and she was delivered to him in a halter, and, on reflecting, as he bought her he thought he had the right to dispose of her as he pleased, in consequence he sold her to the resurrection men and kept the coffin for his sideboard.

Was the poor woman sold to Vaughan? There is no doubt he continued his trade during this time, and his criminal record included a sentence of imprisonment at Brighton for grave-robbing.

In October 1823 there was still no appearance by Vaughan before the Maidstone Court. It was then said he was unable to stand his trial as he was in gaol elsewhere for debt. The Court again declared his recognizances forfeit and a £200 bond entered into by two sureties of £100 were forfeited. These additional recognizances had been imposed at the July Sessions.

Vaughan is believed to have gone next to Manchester and Liverpool from where he shipped bodies back to London. He returned to his old haunts in London around Christmas 1823 but, knowing the police were looking for him for failing to appear at Maidstone, he laid low. Murphy had not forgotten the affair of Holywell Mount nor had he lost his desire for revenge. He heard Vaughan was back in London and set about finding his hiding place. When he discovered it he wrote a letter informing the magistrates where Vaughan was to be found. In consequence, Mr Jones, a Maidstone special constable, was sent to London to arrest him. Vaughan put up considerable resistance but in the end he was captured on Christmas Day. He was taken to Maidstone and put into the Mayor's prison on 26 December, because he was unable to find sureties for his bail. His earlier failure to appear for his trial meant that a total of £400 in recognizances pledged earlier had been forfeited; a fortune in those days.

In January 1824 Vaughan appeared at Maidstone Sessions charged with the theft of five bodies from Maidstone churchyard during the night of 1 November 1821. He was sentenced to two years' imprisonment. On 17th February the *Maidstone Gazette* reported that Vaughan had escaped by sawing through the bars of his cell window and letting himself down by his bedsheets. Three other prisoners in the same cell had made no attempt to get away with him.

Three days later there was considerable commotion among other prisoners, several of whom were desperate characters. Perhaps excited by Vaughan's escape, they had removed iron bars, fixed in a chimney to prevent it being climbed, used them to dig a large hole in the wall and then to force back the bolt of the lock of the prison door. The Mayor, who was also Chief Magistrate, ordered that the ringleaders be caught. After this was done, with some difficulty, he instructed that the recaptured men be put in irons and chained to the floor, in which state they were kept until they promised not to try to escape again.

Vaughan had fled back to Manchester, going, had he known it, from the frying pan into the fire. While there in the latter part of 1823 he had been robbing graves with William Jones Johnson and William Harrison. They had rented a stable in a yard opposite the top of Back King street. Hearing men going out in a gig after dark and returning in the early hours, the neighbours became suspicious that they were engaged in some criminal activity. In January 1824, while Vaughan was being tried in Maidstone and temporarily incarcerated there, one of the Manchester neighbours confronted one of the gang and questioned him about his activities. These enquiries caused the gang to disappear until mid-February when the sound of vehicles was again heard several times going out late at night and returning in the morning. Suspicions were aroused afresh. On Friday 13 February the gig was heard to go out around midnight and return at dawn. During the Saturday morning the men were observed to be very busy in the stable and were seen to carry in three packing cases. The neighbours concluded that the men must have committed a robbery or robberies and thought the police should be alerted before the evidence disappeared. That afternoon the police went to the stable and found two men in the act of fastening the lid on a packing case. Two nailed-up cases were nearby. The three cases were each addressed to a different individual in London. On examining the case not yet nailed-up the police found two human bodies. The men admitted that the contents of the other two cases were of a similar description. The men were taken into custody. The cases were taken to the police office.

The *Manchester Guardian* newspaper of 21st February 1824 reported:

A great ferment has been caused in this town, during the present week, by the detection of two resurrection men, and the finding in their posses-sion of no less than six human bodies recently disinterred.

On Monday they were brought up at the New Bailey before Mr Norris. William Jones Johnson was a good-looking stout young man, well dressed and of tolerably good address: his companion, William Harrison, who seemed to be about forty, of a tolerably respectable appear-ance. When they were called on, Mr Lavender stated the circumstances under which they had been taken into custody. Mr Norris asked the prisoners whence they came and what they had to say for themselves? Johnson, who acted as spokesman for both, replied that he came from London; and that, if the Magistrate would grant him a private examina-tion, he would explain the whole affair to his satisfaction. Mr Norris said he was not in the habit of granting private examinations, except in very particular occasions, and he saw nothing in this case to take it out of the ordinary course. The other prisoner merely said that he came from Liver-pool. Some conversation ensured between Mr Norris and Mr Milne as to the course which should be pursued. Mr Milne observed that he thought the stealing of bodies was undoubtedly a misdemeanour, yet the finding of them in a man's possession was not sufficient to warrant his commitment, unless they were proved to be stolen. Mr Norris said that howevermuch the offence might be involved in matters of science and of general utility, yet it was one which, sitting as a Magistrate, he could not consent to overlook; he should therefore remand the prisoners to give time for enquiry whether any bodies had been missed in the neighbour-hood; he directed Mr Lavender immediately to advertise the circum-stances. The prisoner, Johnson, begged to know what bail would be required, and was answered two sureties in £100 each. He then begged to state, that the other prisoner had nothing to do with the bodies: but the Magistrate told him that they had both been taken dealing with them, and they must both be remanded.

Pursuant to the direction of Mr Norris, advertisements were immedi-ately issued and the bodies, six in number, were exposed to view in one of the rooms at the George Inn, which is now unoccupied. During the whole of Tuesday, crowds of persons, who had recently lost relatives or friends, applied at the Police Office for tickets of admission, to inspect the bodies; but it was not until Tuesday evening that any of them were identi-fied. It was then found that two were bodies of persons who had been interred on the preceding Wednesday in the burial ground of the new Catholic Chapel in Granby Row. On the following morning the remainder were ascertained to have come from the same place.

Their names were:-
Edward Hoare, aged 74, buried Feb.10
Edward Gowry, aged 60, buried Feb.13
Catherine Martin, aged 49, buried Feb.10
Mary Dunn, aged 27, buried Jan.25
Judith Hamilton, aged 14, buried Feb.10
Mary Smith, aged 6, buried Feb.2

On Wednesday the prisoners were again brought up for examination when the relatives of five of the persons whose bodies were found appeared to prove their identity, and that they were buried at the Catholic Chapel.

The prisoners both declined to make any defence. Mr Norris ordered them to find bail to answer at the sessions, themselves in £50 and two sureties in £25 in each case, which sureties, we believe, they have not yet obtained.

On the same evening, about eight o'clock, the bodies having been restored to the coffins from which they had been taken, were again consigned to the earth. The place from which they were stolen is a large grave, calculated to contain from 20 to 30 coffins, and was left with a covering of boards only, until the requisite number were deposited. Of course this rendered it easy to remove the bodies, without leaving any traces which would excite suspicion. The crowd assembled at the re-interment were inclined to maltreat the sexton, whom they suspected of some complicity in the transaction, and Mr Lavender had some difficulty in protecting him from them.

The cases in which the bodies were, were only 2 feet long, 2 feet deep, and 13 inches wide; and in this narrow compass, two full-grown bodies (one, that of a man six feet high) were packed up.

Vaughan arrived back in Manchester to learn that Johnson and Harrison had been detected. Nevertheless he went to St Mark's church and asked a stone-cutter he found working there some questions about a funeral which he said he understood was to take place that day. The stone-cutter replied that no funeral was due in the churchyard that day and suggested that the interment must be going to take place in the Methodist chapel burial ground; but his suspicions being aroused he told the sexton of his concerns. A watch was kept that night on the churchyard and at midnight two men appeared and commenced operations. The watch fired at them and the would-be grave-robbers retreated to another part of the churchyard. They were fired on again and they moved to yet another part. Fired on for the third time, the robbers retreated and escaped unharmed.

When he first learned of Vaughan's escape from gaol, the Maidstone special constable, Jones, went to Vaughan's old haunts in London where, after he had been searching for several days, he received a tip-off that Vaughan had gone back to Manchester. Jones travelled there and sought the aid of the Chief of Police. On the morning after the attempted grave-robbing in St Mark's churchyard, Mr Lavender, a Manchester policeman, with a posse, took Jones to a house behind the Star Inn where they found Vaughan quietly seated at breakfast. As soon as he saw the police, Vaughan ran upstairs to the top of the house. Hearing his pursuers closing in, he made a desperate attempt to dive head-first through a casement window. Although the glass shattered, the iron stanchions with which the window was strengthened were set too close to allow Vaughan's shoulders to pass between them. He put up a fierce struggle but was eventually overpowered and seized. Word that a grave-robber had been arrested spread quickly. On his journey to the New Bailey prison Vaughan was accompanied by hundreds of local people who called, jeered, hissed and shouted abuse. His arrest was another great sensation. As a consequence local burial grounds were examined for signs of desecration. It was found that almost two hundred bodies had been removed from their graves.

Vaughan was returned to Maidstone to complete his two-year sentence and precautionary measures were taken to prevent him escaping again. Mr Jones was widely praised for his diligence in tracing and recapturing such a notorious offender. It is to be hoped that he received the £20 reward that had been offered for Vaughan's recapture.

Johnson and Harrison appeared for trial at Salford Easter Sessions 1824 on three separate indictments of stealing bodies. They pleaded guilty. Johnson told the Court that he had recently failed in business and had a wife and four children, one of whom had been born while he was awaiting trial. He pleaded for a lenient sentence and asked the Court to think of the great distress to which his family would be reduced while he was in prison. Harrison was a pauper who had one child then in the workhouse. Both were sentenced to fifteen months in Lancaster Castle prison.

CHAPTER FIVE

𝒯𝒽ℯ ℳ𝒶𝓈𝓉ℯ𝓇 𝒻𝒾ℯ𝓃𝒹

The next churchyard in which Vaughan was caught operating belonged to the church of St Nicholas, Great Yarmouth, Norfolk. This was the church which Astley Cooper had attended as a boy and young man and in which his father, Dr Samuel Cooper, had been Perpetual Curate. As will be seen, this did not prevent Sir Astley accepting the corpses removed from that churchyard and sent to his agent in London nor financially supporting Vaughan when he was caught.

At the end of September Vaughan, calling himself "Thomas Smith", rented a house and stable in Boulter's Row, Great Yarmouth. He then went to Beccles in Suffolk and engaged William Barber to be his servant.

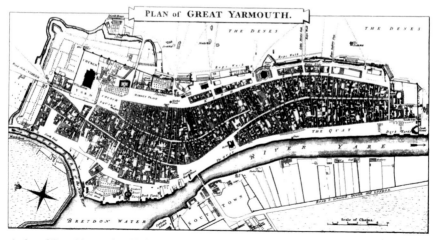

A plan of Great Yarmouth published in 1797. The church of St Nicholas and its extensive graveyard is shown top left .

St Nicholas Church, Great Yarmouth.

When Barber injured his knee, his son Robert was brought from Beccles and employed by Vaughan to help out and look after Vaughan's horse. Vaughan had a horse and a cart for use in his "trade".

All the while using the name "Smith", Vaughan ordered from Job Orris, an employee of Henry Howard, a supply of boxes 2 feet 3 inches in length, 14 inches wide and 14 inches deep, with screw-down lids, which were made and delivered to Boulter's Row. "Smith" also ordered to be made, and bought, two canvas bags from a Mary Clark; he also purchased a supply of sawdust.

With the assistance of the Barbers, he began robbing graves. At the end of November, the Town Clerk of Great Yarmouth and the Deputy Mayor, William Barth, heard rumours of grave-robbing. (According to Bransby Cooper's account it was "in consequence of some imprudent intimacy with a young woman, to whom he represented himself as an unmarried person, that his (Vaughan's) occupation was detected"). They called in the Chief of Police. It was decided to keep watch on the churchyard and catch the criminals at their work. Unfortunately they put the plan into operation without realising that the sexton, Jacob Guyton, was in league with the grave-robbers, and he warned Vaughan who, with the Barbers, made an escape. The sexton was immediately dismissed from his job but he escaped criminal charges.

The rumours of grave-robbing had also got into general circulation locally, causing much anxiety. A Great Yarmouth baker, George Beck, was concerned for the safety of the body of his wife, Elizabeth, who had died in childbirth on 31 October 1827 and had been buried in St Nicholas churchyard on 4 November. He uncovered her coffin, found the lid had been broken open and the body gone. It had been wrapped in a shroud over which had been put a dimity morning gown which had belonged to the deceased. The dress was found lying at the foot of the coffin.

When the news got out the sensation produced was widespread. The churchyard was quickly crowded with townspeople. Wives were seen searching for the remains of their deceased husbands, husbands for their wives, and parents for their children. More than twenty bodies were found to have been taken and the grief of those whose search was in vain can better be imagined than described. Through the natural anxiety of near relations, many bodies left undisturbed by Vaughan were now exposed to view; while everywhere the broken and plundered coffins could be seen.

Observing the distress caused to the relatives of the dead by Vaughan's activities, J.F. Cooper, an onlooker at the scene, in his manuscript "Bodies Stealing from Great Yarmouth Churchyard", called Vaughan "the Master Fiend".

Among the bodies stolen were those of Charlotte Atkins, James Burwell, Elizabeth Beck, Elizabeth Ditcham, Mark Rivett, Eleanor Brightman and her infant son, Roger Burdett, James Rising, Elizabeth Balls and Jane Burrell.

The police officer, Peter Coble, was intelligent and active. On learning that the criminals had fled, he searched the house in Boulter's Row and saw in the stable a quantity of sawdust and tow scattered about as though something had been packed up. His enquiries led him to Beccles, where he interviewed the Barbers. Robert Barber admitted assisting "Smith" and both Barbers were arrested, taken before the Mayor of Yarmouth, who was the Chief Magistrate, and sent to gaol.

Coble tracked Vaughan to Norwich, Colchester and London, where he contacted the officers at Union Hall, the South London Magistrates' Court. Two of the Union Hall officers, Clarke and Read, took Coble to the

White Lion public house in Blackman's Street, Southwark, where they found Vaughan. Officer Clarke said to Vaughan, "Damn it, Tom, you'll be lagged this time. You are charged with stealing a dimity gown as well as the body." Vaughan replied. "Clarke, you ought to know me better than that. If I have taken the body, they will find the gown, no doubt of it, at the foot of the coffin." And so it proved.

Vaughan was arrested and taken back to Great Yarmouth. He was very lucky to be lodged in gaol before local people learned of his capture, for such a sense of outrage, anger and grief at his crime prevailed that he might not have escaped mob vengeance.

Vaughan himself said that, when he was taken to the Court for examination, a crowd collected and threatened to take summary vengeance on him. The magistrates were so fearful he would receive bodily harm that they had him smuggled out of the back door of the courthouse and taken to the gaol so that the examination could take place in safety. In spite of the secrecy surrounding his removal the crowd learned of the move. They pursued him and the officers who had him in custody with such fury that Vaughan believed the mob would have killed him had they caught him.

Although the magistrates were certain he was Vaughan, he steadfastly maintained that his name was Thomas Smith, and so it was in that name that he was committed on 7 January 1828 for trial at Great Yarmouth, with the Barbers. On receiving sufficient sureties for his appearance for trial the following April, the magistrates granted him bail. The entry in Sir Astley Cooper's account book records a payment to a Mr Cock, presumably Sir Astley's agent, "to pay Mr South half the expenses for bailing Vaughan from Yarmouth, and going down £14.7s".

Warned by the keepers of the gaol that it was not safe for him to leave the prison unless he disguised himself, Vaughan somehow obtained the clothes necessary to dress himself as a sailor and in that guise travelled out of Great Yarmouth in a post-chaise. He had to leave behind his horse and cart.

On 1 February he went to Westminster Hall in London and made a sworn statement in support of his request for a writ of *certiorari* to have his case transferred from the Borough Court to the higher Court of the King's Bench. He gave his address as Paragon Court, Newington, Surrey, and described the hatred and hostility he encountered on being arrested. It was still so strong at the time of his release on bail that, he argued, it would not be possible for him to receive a fair and impartial trial at Great Yarmouth, particularly as those disinterred had been relatives or acquaintances of most of the inhabitants of the town. He claimed it was impossible for him to return to Great Yarmouth without danger and risk of his life or at least receiving bodily harm. The deposition was re-sworn on 4 February. On 1 April the indictment was removed by writ of *certiorari* to the Court of the King's Bench. On 3 April Robert Barber agreed to turn King's Evidence against Vaughan and the charges against both Barbers were dropped; they were released from gaol.

Vaughan's case was tried at Norwich Assizes, before Lord Chief Baron Alexander, on 11 August 1828. He was charged with breaking and entering the churchyard of Great Yarmouth, digging and opening a grave and stealing the body of Elizabeth England Beck. There was also a second count on the indictment concerning the body of some person unknown. Mr Alderson and Mr Preston appeared for the prosecution; Mr Serjeant Storks and Mr Kelly for the defendant. Sir Astley noted "a professional friend of mine sent down to liberate him and the amount of his expenditure on this occasion was £160."

George Beck gave evidence of his wife's death and burial. He told the Court how he had examined her grave, found her coffin lid broken and the body gone, and that, together with Officer Coble, he later re-examined the grave and noticed a gown at the foot of the coffin. It was such a one as his wife had had on but he could not swear to its being the same. Coble confirmed the finding of the gown, which was not produced, and said it had been in such a foul state that he had burned it.

Robert Barber told the Court how he came to be working for the defendant and of the night when they had climbed over the churchyard wall. He said he had hidden behind a tomb surrounded by an iron pallisade and kept watch. He testified that he saw Vaughan open a grave, remove the body, put it in a canvas sack they had brought with them and then neatly backfill the grave. Then Vaughan took a body from another grave, put it in a canvas sack and again backfilled the grave.

The bodies were taken to the stable of the house in Boulter's Row, put into two boxes and packed with sawdust. The lids were screwed down, the boxes addressed and marked "glass with care". Barber then borrowed a barrow from a Mr Warren to transport the boxes from the house to the cart which was to take them to London.

Mr Serjeant Storks addressed the jury on behalf of Vaughan before the judge summed up briefly. The jury's verdict was "guilty" on both counts.

Vaughan was remanded in custody for sentence and, on 14 November 1828, was brought up before the Court of the King's Bench. Mr Justice Bayley asked Vaughan whether, as he had no counsel, he wished to say anything for himself. Vaughan pleaded that he had been driven to the crime by distress, that he was sorry for what he had done and that he would never do such a thing again. The prosecutor, Mr Alderson, observed that he did not feel himself called upon to say much in a case of this kind, as it was desirable that it should be kept as much as possible from the public eye. It was a disgusting offence, and their Lordships would please keep in view that this was not a case of a person guilty of one offence of the kind for the purpose of his advancement in science. The defendant was engaged in the business by wholesale, as the hired agent of others. He was not an inhabitant of Great Yarmouth but had been sent from London

Mr Justice Bayley pronounced the judgement of the Court. "Thomas Smith, otherwise Vaughan, you have been convicted of that which is a great offence: the digging out of the grave and taking away a dead body of a female. You say you were driven to it by distress by which I suppose

Norwich Castle, where Vaughan was imprisoned.

you mean pecuniary distress but it appears you had the command of different funds to enable you to carry on this traffic to a great extent, and while you did carry it on, you could not but be aware of the very painful feelings which must be excited by such practices in the minds of the surviving relatives of those whose bodies have been in this manner abstracted. Here is the case of a man who had decently deposited the body of his wife in the grave where, he thought, it would be secure but afterwards he discovers that the body has been dug up and removed by this illegal, and I must say, inhuman practice. However conducive it may be to persons of science, still it is illegal, and most distressing to the feelings of surviving relatives. The judgement of the Court on you is that you be imprisoned in the Castle of Norwich for the space of six calendar months, and that you be committed to the custody of the marshal in the meantime."

In those days time spent on remand in prison was not counted against the sentence of imprisonment. The ten months Vaughan had spent on remand went for nothing and he had to serve six months from the date of sentence in November, during which time he received from Sir Astley Cooper ten shillings a week. Vaughan's wife received a payment on 6 May of 6 shillings.

CHAPTER SIX

Murder for Money

It is interesting to note that selling the dead to the anatomy schools had been going on for decades before it became known that anyone had resorted to murder to supply corpses which being fresh commanded a higher price.

William Burke and William Hare never were bodysnatchers.

William Burke (left) and William Hare.

"Burke's the butcher,
Hare's the thief,
Knox the boy that
buys the beef".

*From a well-known 19th
century verse.*

William Hare and his wife ran a cheap lodging house in Edinburgh. In 1828 Donald, an old Highland lodger of Hare's, died in his bed. He owed Hare £3 in back rent. William Hare and his friend William Burke had the bright idea of copying the bodysnatchers and selling the body to recoup the debt. Recommended to take it to the private school of anatomy run by Edinburgh's most brilliant surgeon, Dr Knox, Hare and Burke were surprised and delighted to be paid £7.10 shillings for it. When another of Hare's old and feeble lodgers, called Joseph, took longer than expected to die of a fever, Burke and Hare helped him on his way by clamping his jaw shut and pinching his nose, causing Joseph to suffocate. They again sold the body to Dr Knox and this time received £10, no questions asked. Burke and Hare proceeded to murder a number of prostitutes and homeless people. They would invite the victim to the house, ply him or her with drink, and when sleep came they killed by clamping shut the jaw and pinching the nose; a method that came to be known as "burking". In all they killed sixteen people, sold the bodies to Dr Knox, and spent their ill-gotten gains on expensive clothes for both murderers and their wives. Although the neighbours noticed the plentiful new finery they did not suspect the source of the new-found wealth.

At the end of October 1828 Hare and Burke threw party to celebrate Halloween. As well as inviting friends to join them in drinking, they invited a beggar-woman, Mary Docherty, and after the other guests had departed they murdered Mary. The next morning the party guests returned to thank their hosts and found Burke acting strangely. He was so insistent that no one should go into his bedroom that the guests became curious and went into the bedroom. There they found Mary's body half hidden in straw on the floor beside Burke's bed. While they went off to inform the authorities, Burke and Hare rushed the body to Dr Knox's school and sold it. The body was later recovered and Burke and Hare were arrested on 1 November.

Because only the body of Mary Docherty was recovered there was no evidence that any of the other sixteen bodies sold to Dr Knox had been murdered. In fact Donald, of course, had died of natural causes. Burke and Hare were charged with murder but the prosecution was doubtful whether a conviction could be obtained with the evidence available and so Hare was persuaded to save himself by turning King's Evidence. Burke was charged with three murders: Mary Docherty; Mary Paterson, a prostitute; and "Daft Jamie" Wilson, an eighteen-year-old boy.

The prosecution decided to try the cases separately and started with the one case in which Dr Knox and his colleagues had not seen the body. It had been seen only by the Dissection Room porter at Dr Knox's school and it was he who appeared in the trial and gave evidence. The authorities in Scotland and England turned a blind eye to the involvement of the medical profession in grave-robbing. It

Dr Knox.

was very rare for a medical person to be charged in connection with the trade.

Burke's common-law wife, Helen M'Dougal, was charged and tried with him. The case against her was found "Not Proven", a verdict only available in Scottish Courts, and she was released. Burke claimed that Mary had died of drink and old age and that the injuries found on her had been caused when the body was doubled up so that it would fit into the tea-chest in which it was carried to Dr Knox's school. It was Hare's evidence which allowed the prosecution to succeed. Burke was found "Guilty" of murdering Mary Docherty and the other charges of murdering Mary Paterson and "Daft Jamie" Wilson were not proceeded with. Thus Dr Knox was not required to give evidence in those cases. Burke was hanged in Edinburgh in 1829. It was supposed to be a public execution but only a small number of ticket holders were present, a fact which so enraged the many medical students in Edinburgh that there was almost a riot, which was avoided when the students were allowed to file past. The next day Burke's partly dissected body was displayed and a crowd estimated at between thirty and forty thousand people came to look. The Edinburgh University Museum became the resting place for Burke's skeleton. Hare was released and set free.

At no time did Dr Knox question the provenance of the fresh bodies that were sold to him and he took the view that he was completely blameless in the whole matter. The public took a different view and his house in Edinburgh was beseiged by large hostile crowds, his windows were broken and an effigy of him was hanged and then torn apart. There were widespread disturbances in Edinburgh expressing public anger and horror. Dr Knox's colleagues ceased to support him and he was shunned socially. He left Edinburgh and moved to London. Unable to get a position he was ostracised and died in poverty in 1862.

CHAPTER SEVEN

Not Guilty

After his release from Norwich gaol in May 1829 Vaughan went to the Colchester area and began working again with his former partner, William Hollis. Together they operated successfully and without detection until February 1830 when Vaughan, still calling himself Thomas Smith, was arrested on suspicion of having been concerned in taking several bodies from burial grounds in Colchester and its neighbourhood. Two Colchester Sergeants of the Mace, W S Cant and J. Edwards, together with other officers, had gone to the Red Cow public house in St James' parish, Colchester, to investigate information received that dead bodies were suspected of being concealed there. The landlady of the Red Cow, Mrs Colleer, denied all knowledge of it and refused to allow the pub to be searched but the officers broke into a locked shed and found the body of an infant, tied up in a handkerchief, lying on the ground. Two more bodies were found hidden in a nearby boxcart. The bodies were taken to the gaol and put on view for identification before reburial. Vaughan underwent two examinations before the local magistrates before being committed for trial. On both occasions he declined to make any defence, saying he was unable to do so without consulting a solicitor.

While he was kept in gaol, a hunt was on for Hollis, who had not been at the Red Cow when Vaughan was arrested, and had escaped. It was not until 30th March that Colchester police officers found him drinking at the Bricklayers' Arms public house in the Kent Road, London. They returned him to Colchester to stand trial with Vaughan at the Colchester Borough Sessions.

Three bills of indictment were found against Thomas Smith (Vaughan) and William Hollis for entering the churchyards of St Mary at the Walls, St Botolph's, and St Andrew's, Greenstead, digging open the graves of Hannah Brown, Christopher Tatum and Mary Ann Roon, and indecently carrying the bodies away. Trial was adjourned to the next sessions.

Hollis, of 22 Thomas Street, Kent Road, in the county of Surrey, petitioned the Court of the King's Bench to have the trial moved from the Borough Court to the higher Court, on the grounds that a fair and impartial trial could not be obtained in Colchester. He said that, on their appearance before the magistrates, his co-accused had pleaded "not guilty" to all counts but that he (Hollis) had, on counsel's advice, refused to plead to any of the indictments. In consequence the magistrates had refused to try either of them and had adjourned the matter. Hollis said his refusal had been to gain time to apply to the King's Bench to take over the trial, because he was certain he could not have an impartial trial in Colchester for two reasons; firstly because several of the magistrates of the Borough Court had expressed themselves with great warmth against him and Thomas Smith and, secondly, because of the prejudices of the greater part of the inhabitants of Colchester.

Henry Whitman, a Colchester surgeon, supported Hollis's application in a sworn statement in which he said that he had informed himself of the feelings of the people of Colchester with regard to William Hollis and Thomas Smith, and of the class in particular out of which the jury for the trial would in all probability be chosen, and he was persuaded that the inhabitants were so prejudiced against the accused that it would be impossible for them to obtain an impartial trial within the borough. A writ of *certiorari* removed the case from Colchester Borough Sessions to the Court of the King's Bench at Chelmsford, Essex, where it was heard at the Assize at end of July 1830.

The three indictments of entering churchyards, digging up graves and carrying away bodies were prosecuted separately. The first case dealt with the charge of disinterring the body of Hannah Brown from St. Mary at the Walls churchyard. Counsel for the prosecution, Mr Adolphus, outlined the case for the Crown saying Smith and Hollis had, for some time previous to the offence in the charge, been staying at the Red Cow in Colchester without, to any appearance, following any kind of occupation and the general impression amongst the neighbours was that they were smugglers. In February it had been found that the body of Hannah Brown, who had been interred the previous day, was missing from the grave. A search was made at the Red Cow public house and in a box cart belonging to the defendants, in which they frequently went out at night and did not return until morning, her body was found. Before Mr Adolphus could call his witnesses to substantiate the charge, the judge, Mr Baron Garrow, intervened. He told the prosecutor that, in his view, it would not be possible to prove, from the circumstances outlined, that the defendants had disinterred the body. That it was found in their cart in the outbuilding of a public house did not prove that the defendants were the ones who dug up the body and put it there. He suggested that as the offence was such a serious one, arousing much public interest, it would be in the interests of justice to proceed with another indictment if there was one with stronger evidence of the Crown's case. Mr Adolphus said he had taken the indictments in the order in which they appeared on the Court List but understood that the evidence in support of the next indictment was stronger and he would adopt the suggestion of the Court. An "acquittal" verdict was therefore returned on the first charge.

The substance of the second indictment was much the same as the first. Smith and Hollis were charged with disinterring the body of Christopher Tatum from Greenstead churchyard where it had been buried on 14 February, while they were living, as described, at the Red Cow. While the grave was being dug, Smith went into the churchyard and enquired who it was for. The morning after the funeral it was found that the grave had been opened and the body taken away. Mr Adolphus said that "the depredators, however, dreading a prosecution for felony, had taken the precaution of leaving behind all the clothes in which the deceased was enveloped". News of the grave-robbing had created a great sensation in the neighbourhood and facts had begun to emerge about the strange lifestyle of the defendants and their cart having been seen standing at the end of the pathway leading to Greenstead church on the morning after the robbery. A search had been made at the Red Cow but no-one could be found except Smith, who had denied all knowledge of the cart, of Hollis and of another man who had been seen with them. On going to the shed it had been found locked and, on its being broken open, Tatum's body was found in a sack box in the cart together with another body.

Several witnesses were called who proved the residence of the defendants at the Red Cow, the burial of Tatum's body and discovery of its loss. Robert Seaman, a Colchester constable, told the Court how he came to find the bodies of Christopher Tatum and others; how he went into the public house and spoke to Smith and the landlady. Told he was to be arrested on suspicion of stealing a dead body, Smith asked "How did this come to get out?" When the constable refused to answer Smith said he "cared nothing about it as it was not for life or death". Telling the Court how Hollis had been arrested in London, Seaman said that Hollis expressed the hope that he would get bail so that he could settle his affairs in case he was sentenced to seven years' imprisonment.

The prosecution case was completed with evidence that a spade, a shovel with a spring handle, a lantern, several pairs of shoes and two coats, all covered with dirt, had been found in the cart; that the cart, with two men on it, had been seen to stop near Greenstead churchyard about 5 o'clock in the morning of 15 February, and that one of them fetched something in sack from behind a blacksmith's shop and put it in the cart.

Mr Broderick, for the defendants, challenged the prosecutions' evidence but, before he could finish his address, the jury intimated they had made up their minds to return a verdict of "acquittal". This decision won the support of the judge who told them they had come to the perfectly correct verdict. He told the Court that he would have put an end to the case himself but for a concern that some of the parties might return to Colchester and say the charge had not been given a fair hearing. "I have no hesitation in saying", he went on, "that this is an extremely suspicious case; in fact I am satisfied in my own mind that the defendants are part of a gang of general body stealers and that they were lurking about the public house for the purpose of carrying away the spoil of different churchyards; but we must have evidence other than this in a Court of Justice. It is not enough that the body is found in their possession; you must be satisfied that they were the parties who actually took it away. I trust that they will be narrowly watched and I hope to see them hereafter sentenced to seven years' transportation." A "not guilty" verdict was then returned.

Mr Adolphus said that as the second charge had failed the prosecution would offer no evidence on the third.

The judge said the Colchester magistrates would have been guilty of scandalous neglect of duty if they had not instituted the proceedings but, though there was no doubt of the defendants' guilt, unhappily the law would not reach them. A "not guilty" verdict was therefore again returned and the prisoners were discharged.

In those days no compensation was available to defendants who had been kept in prison awaiting trial on charges of which they were subsequently acquitted. Otherwise, without doubt, Vaughan would have been quick to ask for a large sum in recompense for the five months he had spent in custody on remand.

So there was Thomas Vaughan in August 1830. He could not go back to London because Murphy was still after him. He could not go back to Manchester, Norfolk, Essex, Kent, Berkshire or the South coast because he was well known to the police. If he wanted to continue his lucrative trade he had to find somewhere where he was not known, where there were plenty of funerals every day, and where there were good communications with London. He decided to investigate the Westcountry.

CHAPTER EIGHT

Unholy Affairs

In 1690 King William III ordered the building of a dockyard on the banks of the Hamoaze river, which separates Cornwall from Devon. A succession of wars meant there was a need for more and more naval ships and so, over the eighteenth century, the dockyard expanded steadily, as did the naval base and associated industries. The town of Plymouth Dock grew rapidly as people from all over England were drawn to the town in the hope of making their fortunes, or at least of getting work that would enable them and their families to lead more comfortable lives. Craftsmen and labourers streamed into Plymouth Dock followed by suppliers of goods of every kind.

On the evenings after the pay frigate had docked and the men had been paid, the town celebrated so riotously that it resembled more a frontier town of the American Wild West than a town in the West of England. Brothels abounded and prostitutes and pickpockets vied with the publicans for a share of the workers' temporary affluence. There were ale houses, gin shops and taverns in such numbers that in one year alone the magistrates closed one hundred in an effort to reduce the drunkenness and violence. Of course, not all the inhabitants joined in the revelry for one visitor described the town as being given over to sin and religion.

At the time of the Domesday Survey there were 25 people living in the manor; by 1832 it had expanded to a population of 34,883. In 1824 the town changed its name from Plymouth Dock, or Dock, to Devonport to distinguish itself from its now smaller neighbour, Plymouth. (Later, in

1914, the three towns of Plymouth, Devonport and Stonehouse amalgamated to form the city of Plymouth.)

The whole of the town of Devonport grew up inside the boundary of Stoke Damerel parish. Ten daughter churches were later carved out of it but when Vaughan came down in 1830 almost everyone born in Devonport was christened in Stoke Damerel, there were hundreds of weddings; it was the Gretna Green of the Westcountry; and almost everyone who died in Devonport was buried in Stoke Damerel churchyard so there were plenty of funerals every day. In fact in 1806 the parishioners had complained to the Bishop of Exeter that they "suffered very great Annoyance, Nuisance and Inconvenience in consequence of the great number of funerals which daily occur" because the entrance porch to the church was stacked every day with coffins awaiting burial.

The view from Mt Edgcumbe over the Hamoaze c.1820, with Devonport visible on the far shore.

Almost all the land on which Devonport was built belonged to the St Aubyn family of St Michael's Mount, Cornwall. Before the Conquest the land, called "Stoches", had belonged to an Anglo-Saxon named Brismar. King William I (the Conqueror) seized the land and gave it to one of his followers, Robert d'Aumale, so "Stoches" became "Stoches d'Aumale" which over time was corrupted to Stoke Damerel. Ownership of the land passed through a succession of families until it was bought in 1667 by Sir William Morice, who had been instrumental, with General Monk, in restoring Charles II to the throne. To complement his purchase of the land the King gave Sir William the advowson, that is the right to appoint a clergyman to the living of Stoke Damerel. The land and advowson came to the St Aubyn family when Sir William's grand-daughter, Catherine, a great heiress in land and money, married Sir John St Aubyn in 1725. Catherine's fortune of £10,000, in half-crown coins, filled two carts when it was taken from her home to her husband's.

The church is first mentioned in the taxation book of Pope Nicholas IV (1288-91) when it practised the Roman Catholic religion as did all churches in England until the time when Henry VIII wanted to marry Anne Boleyn. The church originally had no dedication to a saint and was always, and still is, known as Stoke Damerel church. The oldest part of the church surviving today is the fifteenth century tower. The church was extended to the north in 1715 and to the south in 1751 to meet the needs

Stoke Damerel Church 1787, from a painting by William Payne.

47

of the expanding population. Tradition has it that when in 1750 it was decided that the extension to the south was required, an appeal was made to the Admiralty for funds to carry out the work necessary following of the expansion of the dockyard and naval base. The Admiralty was unable to give cash but supplied ships' knees to be used to support the roof, ships' masts to be used as pillars, cabin doors, and ships' scuttles to be used as windows. The ships' masts being made of New England pine were a soft material which rotted in the damp ground beneath the church and later had to be replaced with oak pillars made on the lathes which shape ships' masts.

The Roll of Rectors dates from 1310 and many good men have served the church and a few not so good. In 1662 all ministers were required to sign an oath of allegiance to the Church of England. John Hickes refused to do so and was ejected from the ministry of Stoke Damerel. His stormy career ended when he was executed at Glastonbury in 1685 for taking part in the Duke of Monmouth's Rebellion. It was for sheltering Hickes that the elderly Dame Alice Lisle was sentenced to death by Judge Jeffreys. Rector Williamson is said to have quarrelled with the congregation and gone out one Sunday after Service, locked the church door and not come back for thirty years. He travelled abroad extensively and in 1794 on a voyage home from Lisbon, where he had gone to benefit his health, he was captured by the French and held prisoner at Quimper, near Brest. While Mr Williamson was away the parish was looked after by the curate, Rev John Hawker, whose father was a well-known preacher and whose nephew was Robert Stephen Hawker, the famous vicar of Morwenstow.

When Mr Williamson died in 1828 the living was offered to 33 year old William John St Aubyn. He was the eldest of the thirteen illegitimate children which Sir John St Aubyn of St Michael's Mount had by a lady named Juliana Vinnecombe whom he did not marry until 1822 by which time the children were grown up. William John is said to have reproved his father for his immoral life and was left out of Sir John's Will in consequence. The living of Stoke Damerel was offered to William John on the understanding that if he took it, he would keep Mr Hawker as his curate for the rest of Mr Hawker's life and allow the Hawker family to continue to live in the parish house. Five days after being inducted into the living the new Rector sacked Mr Hawker, with six weeks' notice, and ordered the Hawker family to leave the parish house. Mr Hawker was a popular and well-loved minister. Many had expected him to have been made Rector and when Mr Hawker announced in church that he had been dismissed hundreds of the congregation were in floods of tears. There was a keen awareness in Devonport of what the French people had achieved for themselves by overthrowing the establishment through Revolution a few years earlier and so there was much anger in the parish about the preference given to the Patron's son and about the treatment of Mr Hawker. Some of the congregation left Stoke Damerel and paid for a chapel to be built for Mr Hawker on a hill nearby, where he preached for the rest of his life.

William John St Aubyn was described by one who knew him as "broad minded, tolerant and by no means strait-laced". He got off on the wrong foot at Stoke Damerel and managed to be at odds with at least some of the parishioners for the rest of his ministry. He is remembered today as "the bad St Aubyn" to distinguish him from his nephew, William St Aubyn, who succeeded him and who is remembered as "the good St Aubyn".

Alice Catherine Young, later Brooke, in her "Childhood Recollections written in Later Life" says she was born in 1851 in a house very near Stoke Damerel church but as she grew up "on Sunday we rarely went to our own parish church because the Rector was a notorious old sinner who would never be tolerated now but when we did occasionally go it interested me very much to hear the old man read the Commandments because I had a vague idea that he had broken nearly all of them. I used to hear many comments on his conduct, especially when he was sent to prison for debt. People always ended up with the same thing; they would shake their heads and say, 'Ah, but he's such a gentleman'." William John St Aubyn died in 1877 aged 83.

While the controversy over the sacking of Mr Hawker was still in people's minds, the "bad St Aubyn" announced that as he owned the freehold of the churchyard he would in future be charging for burials and he published a scale of fees. The parishioners believed that the Patron, Sir John St Aubyn, had given the land for the churchyard and the extensions to it to the parishioners of Stoke Damerel and Sir John, who was a fair and honest man by all accounts, agreed that this was the case. Up to that time burials had been free. Again, there was much anger and the matter came to a head when 23 year old Richard Blackmore died. His father sent to the Rector to ask that the family vault be opened for the funeral. Back came the reply that as soon as the Rector received his fee the vault would be opened. Come the day of the funeral, Mr Blackmore arrived at the church with the cortege and mourners to be met by the Rector, who said that as soon as he received his fee he would instruct the sexton to open the Blackmore family vault. Mr Blackmore refused, saying burial in family vaults had been free from time immemorial. The Rector offered the use of a newly-dug grave without charge but Mr Blackmore was adamant. It was a matter of principle with him. The cortege was turned around and the mourners took the coffin back to Mr Blackmore's house, where a small brick mausoleum was built in the back garden, the coffin put into it, and there it stayed for years while the question of who owned the freehold of the churchyard was fought out in the Consistory Court.

"The bad St Aubyn" was not the only clergyman to "run word". For centuries it was the custom for public meetings of parishioners held in the vestry of the church to vote the amount of a rate to be raised to pay for the upkeep of the parish church. In Reverend W J St Aubyn's time there was much resentment among the growing number of non-conformist followers at the fact that they were expected to pay for the upkeep of the parish church while they had their own chapels to keep in good order. They attended the Vestry meetings and amid much controversy and uproar managed to defeat proposals to raise the rate. The Stoke Damerel Vestry meetings were said to be "the rowdiest in the whole kingdom". In consequence by the time "the good St Aubyn" took over, the church was in a dire state of disrepair. The St Aubyn family paid a lot of money to put the church in a reasonable condition and when the "good St Aubyn's" successsor was offered the living it was made clear to him that it was on condition that he did not come upon the Patron for more money for building repairs or a new church. Having agreed to the terms, two years later the Rector, Reverend Gordon Ponsonby, announced to the Patron that he had had plans drawn up for a new church on glebe land, proposed to make a public appeal for money and thereby put the St Aubyn family under a moral obligation to make a substantial contribution, which they did. Many believed what Mr Ponsonby had in mind was to build a new church suitable to become a cathedral if ever it was decided to make Plymouth a separate See, and, hopefully, himself as the new Bishop. Plymouth was not made into a See with a cathedral and Mr Ponsonby was only able to raise enough money to build a crypt.

CHAPTER NINE

Murder

Soon after 9 o'clock on the evening of Saturday, 21 July 1787, two men, Stephen Hockin and Samuel Organ, were walking through the Mill field on their way from Plymouth to Dock when they heard a cry of "Murder". Another voice was heard to say "Bugger his eyes and blast him" followed by a second faint cry of "Murder". The two men climbed over a stile and, on the bridge at the bottom of Stoke Damerel church-yard, found two hats; one a gentleman's and one a poor man's; and a cane.

As they stooped to examine the items they heard a rustling in nearby bushes and suspecting someone was escaping that way they searched and came across the body of a man lying face down. Hocking cried "I believe here is a gentleman murdered". They turned the body over and tried to raise it but it had no movement and appeared to be dead. Customers of the nearby public house, "Church-house", had also heard the cries of "Murder" and rushed out to assist. One of the newcomers put a hand on the body and found it was still warm. He had read of the means used by the Humane Society for restoring life and he attempted to restart the heart by rubbing it. Near where the body lay Stephen Hockin found a short stick covered in blood. Someone ran to find a doctor and the body was carried to the "Church-house" where another attempt was made to restore circulation by opening a vein but the blood would not flow. A snuff-box found in the dead man's pocket was recognised and the deceased thereby identified as Philip Smith, Second Clerk of the Survey Office in the Dockyard.

Within fifteen minutes of the body being taken to the public house the doctor arrived. He was shocked to see that the murder victim was a friend to whom he had spoken at the churchyard stile only a few minutes before the crime was committed. The doctor tried to bleed the body but without success. On examination of the corpse he found the frontal bone contused over the right eye but no blood had come from that part, and a violent blow had been received across the mouth from which blood had issued. From the appearance of the injuries he deduced they had been caused by a blunt weapon. There was no fracture but the blow on the frontal bone was undoubtedly the cause of death which probably resulted from a concussion of the brain. The two hats, the long thin riding cane and the short blood-stained stick had been brought to the public house. The blood-stained stick was handled by so many people that the blood was rubbed off it before the items of evidence were carried to Mr Justice Blackett. A search of the area for the murderers had been of no avail. However, two possible suspects were clapped into the "Black Hole", as the tiny gaol in Dock was known.

A view toward the Dockyard Entrance in Devonport c.1820

In the early hours of Sunday morning a John Richards called at the home of Mr James Duncan and asked him if he had heard of the murder. "Who's murdered?" asked Duncan. "Mr Smith of the Yard" said Richards. "What Mr Smith the Master?" "No, Mr Smith the Clerk of the Survey Office and I am the man that can swear to the stick that killed him" Richards replied. While they talked Duncan noticed blood on the left side of Richards' blue jacket at the top corner and asked him, "What do you call that?" Richards turned back the corner hastily, as if to hide it, and said, "Poh! Poh! that's nothing". When Mr Duncan saw Richards again an hour later he noticed that Richards had changed his clothes and was no longer wearing the stained blue jacket.

At 3 o'clock in the morning Richards called at the "Black Hole" and spoke to Mr William Pearne. He volunteered the information "I have heard of the murder and if a stick and hat be found, I can swear to them". "Why?" he was asked and replied, "Because one end of the stick is sawed and the other is chopped; and I dare say that the man I saw twice in Five Fields yesterday is the murderer. We have appointed to meet again this morning and if you will, we'll go and seek for him!"

Richards was in Duke Street talking to two boys when Jacob Copplestone came up to the group. Richards at once said to him, "I should know the stick". "What stick?" asked Copplestone. "The stick that Mr Smith was murdered with; and I dare say, the man I saw in Five Fields is the murderer." He then told Mr Copplestone he had seen a tailor there the day before who had a stick under his jacket behind his back. The tailor had been wearing a blue jacket with sugar loaf buttons, black breeches darned upon the knees, and a round hat. Richards said he had met the tailor two or three times on the day of the murder and would recognise the stick because he had noticed it when he and the tailor went to look at the lark's nest. Copplestone accompanied Richards to call upon Mr John Bone. "Mr Bone, I wish I could see the hat and stick; I shall know the stick among ten thousand" Richards said. Mr Bone took them to see the articles which Richards at once identified. "This is the stick, I'll swear before twenty Justices." On being asked how he could swear to it he replied, "Because I saw a tailor, who is a neighbour of mine, twice yesterday in the Five Fields and whilst we were looking for a lark's nest he laid this stick down and I took particular notice of it." He also identified the round hat with the buckle on it as belonging to the tailor.

Copplestone and William Pearne took Richards to the house of the man Richards claimed to have seen in the Five Fields the previous day, Mr William Smith. Richards failed to identify the man and left the house. When asked to take another look at Smith, he refused and said "I said that's not the man".

Later that morning as the landlord of the "Church-house" was discussing with his customers the dreadful events of the previous night, Richards joined them and without preamble announced, "I was in bed at 9 o'clock and it was very lucky I was not outside my own door after bell-ringing". He appeared to be very anxious to convince the company and repeated the remarks to several people. He also mentioned his having seen a man in the Five Fields that day before and his belief that the man was the murderer. His anxiety to establish an alibi for himself before any question of his complicity arose, aroused suspicion. Someone asked him who could prove he was not out after bell-ringing and he replied, "My landlady, Mrs Crouch". The landlord of the "Church-house", Mr G Capron, accompanied Richards to his lodgings where Mrs Couch was asked if she knew that Richards was not out after bell-ringing. "No" she replied. "My wife knows it" said Richards and appealed to that lady to confirm his alibi. "What has your damned blab mouth been talking about?" was her response. "Never mind that" Richards replied, "Where is my jacket?" A blue jacket was produced and witnesses were to say later that they noticed that the top corner of the left side was wet, both inside and outside, as if it had been dipped in water, and part of one sleeve was wet outside only.

Richards was taken in custody to the "Black Hole" but later was released. While he was detained he was visited by Mr Duncan. Before

Duncan could say a word Richards cried out to him, "Don't hang me".

On his release Richards at once returned to the "Church-house" and called for grog. He repeated to all who would listen to him his story of meeting the tailor and added, "If they had let me gone on as they did on Sunday this murder would have been found out but now I'll be damned if it shall. If I am bound to be hanged, I'll hang myself."

Witnesses came forward to say they had seen John Richards and William Smith close to the scene of the crime shortly after 9 o'clock on the evening of the murder. Richards was again taken into custody where he insisted he could prove William Smith was the murderer. William Smith, however, was found to have disappeared. Advertisements offering that "whoever will apprehend the said William Smith shall upon conviction receive Twenty-Five Guineas by applying to Mr Nicholas Hyne, Serge-maker, Plymouth" appeared in the *Exeter Flying Post* newspaper on 2 August. Mr Hyne, who offered the reward, was the deceased Philip Smith's brother-in-law. William Smith was described as "about 27 years of age, 5'7" high, slight made, pale complexion, smooth thin face with little beard, his hair is light brown hanging loose. A married man by trade a Tailor". Smith left Plymouth and made his way to Holcombe Rogus, the home of his wife's parents, near the border between Devon and Somerset. He robbed his father-in-law before leaving and making his way back to Dock, committing several thefts on his journey. On arriving at Dock he found his wife had left their home so he escaped again and made his way back to Exeter, where he enlisted with a recruiting parade under the alias of "Green". He was recognised the same day as a consequence of the newspaper advertisement and arrested.

While Richards was being taken from Dock prison to Exeter gaol, he gratuitously informed his captors that he was of the opinion that the murder weapon was a broomstick with the pointed end sawed off and the other end chopped off, although he knew Mr Bone was of the opinion that the murder weapon was a sapling. On close examination being made of the small stick found near the murdered man, Richards' descrip-

The grounds outside the newly-built Exeter Goal c.1820.

tion was found to fit exactly. Richards was held at Exeter for some days before Smith's arrest.

Mr Copplestone travelled from Dock to interrogate the prisoner at Exeter gaol. At first Smith insisted his name was Green and denied he had ever been in Dock. Copplestone told him he knew positively to the contrary because they had both lived in the same neighbourhood and although they had never spoken Copplestone knew Smith by sight. Smith abandoned the pretence, admitted he was Smith, and made a statement giving his version of the fateful events. He said he and Richards had met three times on 21 July. The third time they met under the Royal Naval Hospital wall about nine in the evening. Richards had said that if they met the man who had injured him he would have his revenge that night. They crossed the bridge at the bottom of Stoke churchyard and, having occasion to ease himself, Smith jumped over the wall into the meadow. On rejoining Richards he found him standing on the low parapet of the bridge with his back against the churchyard wall. Smith stood in the roadway opposite to Richards for three or four minutes before Richards said, "Damn him, here he comes". Smith looked and saw Mr Philip Smith, a universally respected man, on his way home from the Dockyard to his home in Plymouth by way of Stoke churchyard and the Five Fields. He had a strong preference for that route, over the road through Stonehouse, because his father had always walked that way. As Philip Smith drew level with Richards, Richards stepped forward and struck a back-hand blow on the face with a stick with such force that Richards lost his balance and reeled into William Smith causing him to fall and lose his hat. William Smith claimed he got up and ran away without touching the victim. On a subsequent examination William Smith admitted that the fragment of cloth could have come from a shirt of his but claimed his wife had torn the ruffle off his. He also identified as his articles of clothing taken from his home; a blue jacket with sugar-loaf buttons and a pair of breeches darned at the knee. He denied knowing there was blood on the front of the jacket and under the collar behind, and could not explain how the jacket came to be blood-stained.

The prisoners were then brought face-to-face. They agreed they had met in the Five Fields on the day of the murder. Smith accused Richards "You are the man who killed Mr Smith". "No", replied Richards, "I saw you in Five Fields with your jacket buttoned and I believe you had the stick behind your back". Through all examinations Richards maintained his innocence and denied being out of doors on the evening of the murder, but the black hat with red paint on it proved a distinctive identi-fication.

John Richards and William Smith were charged with murder and tried at Exeter in March 1788 before Mr Justice Buller. When the jury were called Richards expressed the wish that no inhabitant of the parish of Stoke Damerel should be allowed to serve. As no such persons were among those called, none of the jury were challenged. Both prisoners pleaded "not guilty".

The prosecution opened its case and called witnesses who described having seen Richards and Smith in the Five Fields on 21 July at 5 p.m.

when Richards was carrying a stick similar to the murder weapon; at 8 p.m. when Richards was wearing a round black hat with red on it and concealing something beneath his blue jacket; and just after the firing of the 9 o'clock gun when they were seen by Mrs Ann Welsh near the bridge at the bottom of Stoke churchyard where the murder had been committed, Richards still wearing his black hat with red paint on it.

Richards' landlady, Mrs Jane Couch, gave evidence which destroyed his alibi. She said she saw him at home on 21 July at 6.30 in the evening but later he went out by the back door and she did not see him again until 8 a.m. on the 22nd when he came to her room to ask her if she had heard about the murder. As she had not heard he told her about the murder "committed last night just after 9 o'clock". "I know perfectly well who did it", he told her, before reminding her that he had been at home the previous evening and had not gone out after bell-ringing. "I told Richards that he went out of the back door after he came home in the evening and he seemed to be confounded" she testified. Richards called out to her from the dock that she was a wicked woman to tell such lies and swear his life away. "My Lord", she says I came to her room at 8 o'clock but that cannot be; because I was in custody at 7 and I desire Mr Hyne, the deceased's brother-in-law be called; he can swear I was in custody before the time she mentions." The Court told him Mr Hyne would be examined on that point later. Mrs Couch commented, "Sure, Richards, I speak nothing but the truth, 'twas 8 o'clock". Questioned on her knowledge of a hat worn by Richards, Mrs Couch said, "He had a black hat and there was red paint on the top of it". Richards asked her "After you came from the Justice did you not say that I had shoved you and that you now had it in your power to be revenged of me?" "No", Mrs Couch replied, "you pushed me against the chimney about a year ago and I was offended at it but have no ill-will against you because I cannot say you did it purposely."

Mr Wilmot Mason and Ann Warsley, who lived in the same house as William Smith, were called to give evidence as to the ownership of the hat with a velvet band and a buckle found at the murder spot. Both said it belonged to William Smith. A Mr James Grills gave evidence relating to a conversation he had had with Richards in May 1787 when Richards complained that Mr Smith of the Survey Office had had him dismissed from the Dockyard and swore, "I'll be damned if I don't be revenged and break every bone in his body if I can but catch him in a place where." Richards protested Grills had committed perjury for it was impossible they could have spoken in May as he was in the country working at rinding of wood in May. Grills admitted he could have been wrong about the date but insisted Richards had made the threat as he had sworn.

Mr Nicholas Hyne was sworn in to answer Richards' question, "Mrs Couch says I was at her house after 8 o'clock – was I not in custody by 7?" Mr Hyne said, "I was so hurried at my brother-in-law's death I cannot speak positively as to time but I believe it to have been after 8 o'clock".

The Court then advised the prisoners, "You have heard the evidence that has been given against you and now is the time for you to enter upon your defence".

Smith's defence was, "My Lord, I know nothing about this affair. I had no hand in the murder. I came from London and had not been in Dock above six weeks. I saw Richards twice in the Five Fields, and I met him the third time under the Hospital wall. He said if he met Mr Smith that night he would be damned if he would not be revenged of him. He went away over the bridge and that's all I know of the matter." Asked whether he had any witnesses, Smith replied, "No".

Richards began his defence, "My Lord, I was not out of my house after 6 o'clock. The people of Dock and round about are all against me. What they have sworn is as false as God is true, and if I die for this, I shall die an innocent man". When the Court asked whether he had any witnesses, Richards replied, "Yes. Where's Mr Bartlett?" His Counsel called, "Stop! Where is your attorney? I would consult him before Mr Bartlett is sworn." Richards' Counsel held a whispered consultation with Mr Bartlett after which he whispered to Richards for two or three minutes. Richards then declined to call any witnesses and rested his defence on his own unsupported assertion of innocence.

Mr Justice Buller then summed up for the jury. He told them the evidence, as it respected each of the prisoners, was different in its nature and it would therefore oblige him to spend more time than usual in summing it for their consideration.

He would separate one part from another accordingly as it affected either of the prisoners distinctly and, having done so, the jury would return a verdict as to the guilt or innocence of the prisoners individually. First as to Richards. He noticed what had been deposed concerning the extreme anxiety to exculpate himself when he had not been accused; his sayings respecting his luck in being at home; the nicety of the third meeting, his critical description of the stick, his continual talk of the murderer, his chagrin at being shown the blood on his jacket, the hasty washing of it, his saying, "Don't hang me" and that if bound to be hanged he would do it himself; his confusion at Mrs Couch's declaring him to have gone forth at the back door; his being seen by different witnesses going toward and at the place of murder almost at the minute of its commission, strengthened by the circumstance of the hat with red on it, his early call at the "Black Hole", and his profession of malice towards the deceased – all of which the jury were to consider and account for and deliver a verdict accordingly.

The jury, after two minutes consultation, returned a verdict of "Guilty".

As to Smith, the Judge advised the jury, the question lay in a smaller compass; his hat and part of his shirt had been found on the place of murder and he confessed himself an eye-witness of the attack. It was for consideration then whether he knew of its being intended or had assisted in it, and it should be remembered that according to his own account he accompanies Richards after he has declared his resolution to be revenged on the deceased if he meets him that night; and that when Richards is on the wall he stands opposite him in the way for some minutes but for what purpose he has not said. The jury would therefore consider that he had mentioned his rising and running off during the scuffle, this was somewhat inconsistent as by the account he had given no scuffle had taken place when he ran off. The jury would therefore weigh the whole and find a verdict according to their best discretion.

The jury conferred for about fifteen minutes and the foreman told the Court that eleven only agreed. He was informed that they must all agree, and in a minute they again returned a verdict of "Guilty".

Judge Buller then proceeded to pass the sentence, and delivered a speech that was said to have drawn tears from the eyes of many who heard it, particularly from those who had known the murdered man. He ended his speech saying, "You, John Richards, have shown you possess a heart susceptible of the blackest malice. You long harboured and cherished the murderous thought and anxiously sought an opportunity to execute the purposes of your diabolical revenge.

As for you, William Smith, though it has not here appeared what were your motives to the commission of so diabolical a crime, yet enough has been unfolded to prove that you wanted not an inclination to become an accomplice with anyone in an undertaking, however desperate and bloody.

Such is the form of the Law that in the sentence which I am bound to pass, your bodies must after death be ordered for dissection. But although I am obliged to pronounce this judgement yet it shall not be so, for in the disposal of your bodies after execution I shall consider them as monuments of the fate which must ever attend iniquities like yours and they shall be suspended between Heaven and earth a spectacle of horror.

The time that remains to you in this world is very short indeed and your sufferings here can be nothing compared to those which must be expected to await crimes like yours at the unerring Tribunal of the Judge Omnipotent before whom you must soon appear. Employ therefore the moments that are left you in deprecating his vengeance and prepare yourselves for divine mercy by the most sincere contrition.

The gibbet at Stoke Damerel churchyard (from a contemporary sketch).

The sentence of the Law is, and I therefore order that you be taken to the place from which you came and from thence on Monday next to the place of execution; there to be hanged by the necks until you be dead; and that your bodies be delivered to a Surgeon to be dissected and anatomised and may the Lord have mercy on your souls."

Into the silence which followed, the Court ordered, "Gaoler, take back the prisoners".

John Richards, who was considered to be a person of extreme ignorance, appears to have been a thoroughly bad character and a blood-thirsty, vengeful person. He had worked in the Dockyard as the rope-maker's labourer and was discharged for neglect of duty, after which he served aboard a man-of-war in the capacity of butcher. A few years before the murder, he received some offence from a sentinel on duty in one of the squares in Dock Barracks and he threatened to be revenged. The next time the sentinel was on duty at the same post he was murdered by some unknown hand. Richards was strongly suspected. On another occasion, without any provocation he broke his wife's arm by dashing it violently across his knee. He later nearly killed a shoemaker during a quarrel. The shoemaker was only rescued just in time to save his life. He had been reduced to a state of insensibility by Richards' efforts to strangle him.

William Smith was a tailor by trade who came from the neighbourhood of Wellington, in Somerset. During his stay in Dock he is said to have "lived in a very loose manner being observed to go in and out of his lodgings at all hours of the night, and frequently quarrelling with his wife". It is most probable he was induced to assist in the murder by Richards promising him as a reward the watch, money and other property which might be found on Mr Philip Smith's person.

In those days there was no Court of Appeal for criminal cases, in fact not until over 100 years later, so in spite of his continued denials of any knowledge of the murder, two days after the sentence Richards was taken with Smith, and other criminals under sentence of death, to the Heavitree Gallows at Exeter. A huge crowd gathered to see the executions and Richards cried out to them of his innocence. He kept up his protests until their arrival at the fatal tree where an eye-witness described Smith's behaviour as "penitent and becoming to their unhappy situation" but that of Richards bordered more on insanity, he harangued the populace for nearly an hour with a seeming insensibility to the awful approach of death. He insisted on dying without a hood on his face which he would not permit to be put on, and it being noticed that he was not pinioned sufficiently to prevent him raising his hands, he told the executioner, he would put them in his breeches pocket from where he would never again take them and which he instantly did. Richards desired that Smith be asked if he (Richards) was innocent. It was done and Smith having declared Richards' innocence, they were both launched into eternity. Later that night the bodies were cut down. Although he had been bound to pronounce an order for dissection, the Judge had used his discretion to vary it to gibbeting so Richards' and Smith's bodies were put in a cart to be taken back to Plymouth Dock while the others hanged were sent for dissection.

On Easter Tuesday 1788 a crowd of thousands assembled around the transverse gibbet set up below the churchyard, on that side of the banks of the creek near where the murder had taken place, to watch the bodies taken from the cart, each put into iron cage and hung by chains from the arms of the gibbet. Two thousand copies of a pamphlet "A Genuine Account of the Trial" were said to have been sold to those waiting around the gibbet.

The church had always stood isolated, surrounded as it was by fields and open land, and now the bodies, rotting in the creaking chains caused it to become a notorious place to be given a wide berth when possible. For seven years the bodies hung there, with flesh decomposing, birds flying in and out of the cages pecking at them, until the cage containing the remains of Smith was seen to fall down, with its irons and head and swivel, by Mr Nicholas Hyne. It was interred under the gibbet on the Sunday morning following. The other body, Richards', hung there longer, rotting with fragments dropping off. Then it disappeared. How was never known. Probably it fell at high water and being in an advanced state of decomposition might have been carried off by the receding tide. Eventually wind and water rotted the base of the gibbet itself. On 18 September 1827 it was blown down and fell into the creek. It was carried downstream by the ebbing tide. It was floating past Hawkin's shipwright's yard when it was spotted by some apprentices who drew it ashore. Subsequently an enterprising local carpenter did a roaring trade in snuff boxes made from the wood. Prints of the scene at Millbridge showing the bodies hanging from the gibbet close to the church, were popular and a Christmas card was also produced later bearing the unseasonal scene.

One story has it that a stone in the churchyard wall was stained when the ill-fated Mr Philip Smith's brains were knocked out and this excited much morbid curiosity until it fell out of the wall in 1841. It is said that the stain was periodically freshened up by a touch from the brush of passing apprentice painters.

CHAPTER TEN

For the Last Time

When Vaughan arrived to reconnoitre the possibilities Devonport offered, he would have found that, in addition to a steady supply of new corpses each day, Stoke Damerel churchyard had even more attractions. The church was still standing isolated on the banks of the creek where boats could go down river to where steamers plied regularly to London. Starting not far from the church, there was also a swift stage coach service between Devonport and London. Apart from four houses, called Millpleasant, near the eastern end of the churchyard, the churchyard with its high wall and metal gates was still surrounded by undeveloped land. Best of all from Thomas Vaughan's point of view was the fact that nobody would go anywhere near Stoke Damerel churchyard after dark. Although the gibbet had blown down in 1827, when Vaughan came in 1830 memory of the horrors of the gibbet was still so vivid that people continued to pass by quickly during the day and shun the area after dark. People did not care to pass through the dark pathfield that led to the narrow solitary road which ran past the church to Plymouth. The notoriety of the churchyard had been reinforced when, in 1810, a saucer-eyed ghost was reported to be haunting it. The ghost was said to be that of a recently deceased waterman whose spirit was anguished by the speed with which his widow had found consolation with a local baker.

Appreciating how good a place this was for him to do business, Vaughan, now calling himself Thomas Goslin, took a house, number 4 Millpleasant, close to the churchyard wall and sent for his wife, Louisa. When they were established in their new home he procured two men from

London to assist him; Richard Thompson and John Jones. Thompson brought his wife, Mary, and the five of them set up home in the house.

Of course the other inhabitants of Millpleasant had no idea "the Master Fiend" had moved in. They saw a prosperous looking man of 39, 5'4" tall, with grey eyes and brown hair, and with a pretty wife ten years his junior and three servants. So Vaughan began robbing the churchyard of Stoke Damerel and sending the dead of Devonport to the London anatomy schools until the day when the neighbours became suspicious.

Bransby Cooper says that "the gang lived together for some months unsuspected of any illegal practices but Vaughan's vicious habits at last led to their detection for after a time he began to pay court to the female servant of a family living opposite the house. The girl, however, not only turned a deaf ear to his entreaties but began to suspect some ill intention in the whole party. She determined closely to watch their proceedings and having discovered fresh reasons to doubt their respectability, informed her master of her suspicions. This gentleman, his curiosity being aroused, himself now observed their movements and soon felt

The Victualling Yard at Devonport. A scene that would have been familiar to Thomas Vaughan.

convinced that love of retirement, which was stated as their reason for coming to this sequestered spot, was not the only motive for their residence and even thought there was sufficient ground to place them under the surveillance of the Police." He revealed his suspicions to the authorities, stating his belief that the party had come down for the purpose of smuggling.

A person by the name of Richard Ellis, a former London Bow Street officer, had recently been appointed head of the Police, and he at once investigated the matter. Disguising himself, he went, on the following day, to the dwelling of the suspected individuals and, after sauntering around for some time, recognised Vaughan as a London bodysnatcher without himself being observed by any of the party.

Finding that two funerals were to take place the next day, Tuesday 9 November 1830, Richard Ellis went to Stoke Damerel churchyard. In the eastern churchyard he observed a man, later found to be Richard Thompson. In the path leading down between the two western parts of the churchyard he saw a young woman, later found to be Mary Thompson. Soon after he saw both of them on that path talking together. A few minutes later Richard Thompson went away across the field called Church Field, towards the Church-house inn leaving the young woman standing there. Ellis moved to the northern part of the churchyard where he had a good view of the houses at Millpleasant. Shortly afterwards he saw Richard Thompson run up by the wall at the back of the houses and enter the fourth back door. A little while later Ellis went to the church and saw two coffins carried in. When they came out of the church he watched as the coffins of the eighteen-year old girl, Eliza Hanger, and the fifty-four year old man, Thomas Webb, were put into their graves. He saw Mary Thompson approach and talk to the people who were standing around one of the graves and heard her asking what the poor creature had died of and how old she was. She remained at the grave for about five minutes and then went to the eastern part of the graveyard where the other coffin had been interred. Again he saw her in conversation with the

St Michael's Terrace, Stoke Damerel c.1820. The gentility of the lives of those living in the newly constructed terrace would have contrasted greatly with the shocking robbing of graves at the nearby churchyard.

mourners. She strolled about the churchyard for another five minutes before he saw her leave by the same gate as Richard Thompson and go across the field to the Church-house Inn. He watched her return the same way and go down the hill towards Millpleasant. She walked on the Mill bridge and waited five or six minutes before going up the hill towards Plymouth and away from Stoke.

Richard Ellis returned to Devonport and sent for two of his constables, James Day and Roger Halse. Between 7 and 8 o'clock the same evening he accompanied constables Day, Halse and Ambrose Nosworthy to a field at the back of Millpleasant. With Halse and another constable called Pike, he went into a garden near the north-east corner of the churchyard where for two hours they waited in the cold darkness of that eerie place before they heard a noise in the churchyard as of a person shovelling. It appeared to come from the direction of the spot where he had seen a body buried during the day. The noise continued at intervals for half an hour before the waiting men heard something heavy fall, seeming to be near the eastern churchyard wall. A minute later they heard another heavy fall. In spite of the darkness of the night, about two or three minutes afterwards, they saw a man come out by the side of a hay ride which adjoined the churchyard. The man went in the direction of Millpleasant scanning the side of the hedge as he did so, so that Ellis gained the impression that the man was looking to see if anyone was coming. As he went towards the back of the house at Millpleasant there was just sufficient light for Ellis to make out his size. He judged him to be John Jones, otherwise known as Quinn. He continued to watch but saw no-one else and eventually returned to Devonport, leaving two men to keep the house under observation.

Just before dawn the following morning Ellis and his men returned to Millpleasant and, while Ellis took position at the back door of the property he had earlier seen Thompson enter, the others went around to the front of the house. At about a quarter to seven Ellis and Nosworthy got over the back wall, ran through the garden and got in position at the rear of the house. The back door was very quietly tried but proved to be locked. Nosworthy knocked at the door while Ellis lifted the window of the back parlour. Immediately the window was lifted John Jones came to it. His coat was off and he was only partly dressed. Ellis told Jones that he was searching for soldiers who had deserted and ordered him to open the door.

Jones quickly turned away and hurried off without saying anything. Nosworthy jumped into the house through the open window and opened the back door. Ellis entered and immediately went to the kitchen where he saw two sacks lying on the floor in the middle of the room. He could see, through a hole in one of the sacks, a part of a human body. A search of a cupboard in the same room yielded a piece of cloth in which were contained a great number of human teeth and a turnscrew, while in another cupboard in the parlour piles of grave clothes were found. By this time the other officers had entered and arrested all five occupants, who were in a state of undress.

Vaughan's main concern was for his possessions. He asked Ellis to have care taken of the furniture and the house for all of it was his. The five were arrested and taken to Devonport prison. With them safely locked up, Ellis went to Stoke Damerel burial ground to superintend the opening of the newly-made graves. He found that the corpses which had been interred on the previous day were missing. The screws at one end of the coffins had been taken out and the lids forced up. Most of the grave clothes had been left behind.

Later that same day the five prisoners were taken before the magistrates, Mr Edmund Lockyer and Captain Samuel Pym RN. So strong was the feeling aroused against the gang that it was necessary to take the precaution of bringing them from the gaol between a double row of constables, to prevent their being attacked by the huge crowd which had assembled to see them. It had to content itself with hissing and shouting abuse. The accused were all strangers to the crowd, having moved into the parish just some months before. Only Jones was recognised by some present who had seen him at public sales in the capacity of servant to Louisa "Goslin".

A deep impression was made on the crowd by the respectable and prosperous appearance of the well-dressed defendants. Vaughan's well-cut black coat was particularly noted as he expressed to the magistrates his anxiety for the safety of his house and goods and his objection to his wife being taken into custody.

In Court, depositions of the witnesses were taken, signed and witnessed by the magistrates. The defendants were all committed to stand trial at the Devon General Quarter Sessions at Exeter, and later that night were transferred to Exeter gaol. Despite the lateness of the hour when they left, several hundred people followed the vehicle from the prison to the outskirts of town, trying to get at the prisoners but having to content themselves by shouting threats and abuse.

The *Exeter Flying Post* of Thursday 18 November 1830 reported that the news of the grave-robbing had spread around the parish like wildfire:

People hurried in crowds to the church-yard which soon became a scene of desolation and misery beyond the power of language to describe. The Rector, with a sympathy for the afflicted friends and relatives of the dead highly honourable to his character, afforded every facility for the examination of the recently formed graves. Numbers were employed in digging up the newly-interred dead for the purpose of satisfying the agonised feelings of the living. Nine coffins were found emptied of their contents and in many instances it was discovered by the position of the bodies that the dead had been disturbed in their graves though not carried off in consequence, it is supposed, of their being too much decayed. The grave-digger having been seen drinking at a public house in company with the men has been taken into custody and lodged in gaol. It is generally supposed that the gang exported the bodies immediately on their being raised for London by steam packets which go to and fro weekly between Devonport and London or sent them by coach. At high water boats can approach within a few feet of the church-yard wall. (The Rector referred to was the "bad St Aubyn".

The discovery that several bodies had been decapitated and the heads taken added to the widespread feeling of horror. The bodies of Miss Hanger and Mr Webb were quietly re-interred.

Although their real surname was known to the authorities, the Vaughans were tried under the alias "Goslin" and referred to as "Goslin" in newspaper reports and official records for the next eight years (and for the rest of their known lives).

CHAPTER ELEVEN

The Trial

On Tuesday, 7 December 1830, at the General Sessions held in Exeter, Thomas Goslin aged 40, Louisa Goslin aged 30, John Jones alias Quinn aged 27, Richard Thompson aged 23 and Mary Thompson aged 20 stood trial on a charge of disinterring two dead bodies from the burial ground at Stoke Damerel. Those were the bodies of Miss Eliza Hanger, an 18 year-old girl who had lived near the Timber Pound, Devonport, and Thomas Webb, a 54 year-old man who had lived in Garden Street.

Nicholas Wood, aged 63, a grave-digger of the parish of Stoke Damerel was charged with having counselled, procured and incited the other prisoners in the disinterment and carrying away of two dead bodies.

All but Wood were charged with stealing a shift from the grave of Charity Netting deceased, the property of her legal representative, and further charged with stealing a pair of white cotton stockings, the property of the legal representative of Thomas Webb deceased.

The prisoners pleaded "not guilty" to all charges and the prosecutor, in outlining his case said to the jury, "if an individual, whom I will suppose to be a surgeon, in the prosecution of his studies thought it proper to dig up a corpse it was most likely he would have no intention of stealing a pair of stockings, his object being not to gain any pecuniary advantage by disinterring any part of the grave clothes but if, on the other hand, individuals employed by others for this purpose and making a livelihood not only by supplying the medical profession with subjects but also taking an opportunity of plundering the corpse, then they become guilty of the felony". He told the jury that what they would have to try was whether the prisoners took the bodies for the purpose of making a profit from this alone or appropriated parts of the grave clothes for the purpose of making a profit from them also.

In law, for a felony charge to succeed, it is necessary that the thing taken or stolen should possess value and that there should be someone standing in relation of owner of the stolen thing. As it was held that a body could not be said to possess any value, and no-one could be produced to say he or she was its owner, it was not possible for a felony charge to be brought when a corpse was stolen. A lesser charge of misdemeanour applied. However, grave clothes, such as stocking and shifts, did have value and did belong to the administrators of the deceased person's estate. Therefore the more serious crime of larceny would apply, carrying a higher penalty. The woman's shift stolen from the body of Charity Netting technically belonged to her son, William Netting, and the stockings to Thomas Brooks, although there was some doubt about who owned what until letters of administration of the effects of the deceased had been taken out.

Therefore the charges also named as owners the Reverend W.J. St Aubyn, clergyman of the parish; the Archdeacon of Totnes and Christopher Lord, Bishop of the Diocese, on the basis that until letters of administration were taken out the property belonged to the deacons and ordinands of Exeter Diocese.

When the prosecutor had outlined his case he called his witnesses. Richard Ellis told the Court of the events of 8-11 November, of his keeping watch on the churchyard, his discoveries at Millpleasant and the arrest of the prisoners.

He said the most curious discovery was that of a letter found on Mary Thompson addressed to "Dear Goslin" and signed "Thomas Davis". After acknowledging receipt of several packages with "things" and desiring no more should be sent for the present, as he had no more orders, and mentioning several pecuniary arrangements between the parties, the writer summed up with an account of the current position.

The account (as published in *The Alfred* of 23rd November 1830) read as follows:-

	£. s. d.
On first account left due to you	1. 11.10
September 20th 2 heads £1.5s. carriage 5s. 4d	0. 19. 8
22nd 2 heads £1.5s. '' 5s. 4d	0. 19. 8
25th 3 heads £1.2s '' 5s.10d	2. 0. 0
	6. 7. 4
25th Paid Mr Ealing	10. 0
	5. 17. 4
27th Remitted	5. 0. 0
Left due	17. 4

(Either Mr Davis was a poor arithmetician or the newspaper contained typographical errors.)

The Alfred article also mentioned that 13 bodies had been found missing. It went on:-

A letter has been received by Ellis from one of the officers at Union Hall, London, stating the prisoner Goslin's real name to be Vaughan and that he is known to all the London police. Several pawnbroker's duplicates, in the name of Vaughan, were found on the person of Louisa Goslin which confirm the statement in the letter received by Ellis.

Ellis said that on the way to prison in Devonport he had remarked to Richard Thompson that he ought to get a living in a better way than stealing dead bodies. Thompson had replied, "Why it is a pity that after people had been at the expense of getting their friends decently buried they should be disturbed but you know we get by it". He added that he had not been involved in such ransacking more than a week and he would take care this should be the last.

Ellis finished his evidence by confirming that he had found two dead human bodies, a male and a female, each in a sack, on the floor of the kitchen at the house in Millpleasant and that he had had the bodies put into a cart and left there in the charge of Constable Halse.

Constable Ambrose Nosworthy said that he went to 4 Millpleasant where he saw the prisoner Quinn, otherwise Jones, who said to him, "This is a bad job and I suppose they'll turn me up for it". Nosworthy asked him what he meant and Jones replied that he supposed he could be transported for at least seven years for the crime and that if he had not been drunk he would not have done it. He wished he had remained at home in his lodgings and would rather have been shot than have disgraced himself in this manner.

Constable James Day related how, at about 8 o'clock on the night of Tuesday 9th November, he stationed himself in a field at the back of Millpleasant where he remained until 11 o'clock when he twice heard a noise, apparently the sound of iron instruments knocking one against another. About a minute later he saw three persons moving by the end of the wall which faced the north boundary of Millpleasant at the back of the house. Two of them appeared to have lighter-coloured clothes and seemed to be loaded with something but he could not say what it was. He went on to tell how he saw them go in at the back door, the fourth up by the wall, which he now knew to be the door to the house where the prisoners were apprehended. Directly they passed in he saw through a window a light moving in the house. The next morning he went with Nosworthy, Halse and others to the house where he had seen the men go in. He placed himself at the front door with Halse and two watchmen. Soon after 7 o'clock he heard a noise in the house and the window shutters were thrown open. At that moment he saw Jones, otherwise Quinn, attempt to climb out of the window. On seeing the constable Jones moved back and Day jumped in after him, secured him, and left him in charge. Day then went upstairs into the front room where he found Thomas and Louisa Goslin, and Richard and Mary Thompson. Thomas and Louisa jumped out of bed as Day entered, while Mary Thompson got up from a bed by the side of the Goslins' bed. Richard Thompson was found under the bed and had to be repeatedly asked to come out before he did so. Constable Day then ordered all four to dress. He said that on the washstand in the back room he found about 100 human teeth. The prisoners were taken into custody. On their way to prison an onlooker, pointing at Louisa Goslin, asked, "Has that woman been stealing bodies?". She replied, "Yes, and I will again as soon as I get rid of this (charge) I will do it again".

Day identified a quantity of screws found in the kitchen where the bodies were and identified them as screws used in closing down coffins. The heads of the ones he showed had dirt on them. He also produced a quantity of packing cord which he had found in the back room.

He said that on the Thursday, 11th November, he had returned to 4 Millpleasant and found, on a chair in the back parlour, a shift which he produced to the Court. It had been quite wet when he found it. Before the prisoners had been taken from the house on the Wednesday, Day had locked the door of the room where the shift was found and had then fastened the front and back doors before he left. Thomas Goslin asked him to take care of the property in the house and said it was his. When Day returned on the Thursday everything in the house was in the same state. He also said that since her arrest Louisa Goslin had told him that the shift in question was hers.

Constable Roger Halse gave evidence that he went to the house at Millpleasant on 10th November where he found the prisoners, the Goslins, the Thompsons and Jones. He took them into custody, after which he locked the house and took the key in his pocket. He returned to the house on the Thursday, in company with Jane Chapman, who found some stocking, of which he took possession. He said that on the Wednesday all five prisoners had been in the room where the stockings were found. Goslin had said that it was his house and furniture and requested that the furniture might be taken care of. Halse confirmed that he took the bodies found in the kitchen to the workhouse where he gave them into the governor's charge.

James Lancaster, governor of the parish workhouse, gave evidence that he had received from Roger Halse two sacks containing two human bodies, one male and one female. He had shown the male body to Jane Chapman who had identified it as that of Thomas Webb. It had on its left foot a piece of cloth. He had the cloth taken off and a wound on the sole of the foot was exposed. A good deal of matter, which he supposed to be the discharge from the wound, was on the cloth. He afterwards gave the cloth to Jane Chapman.

James Hanger, Eliza's father, and William Rowe, who made her coffin, both testified that they saw her body put in its coffin and saw the lid screwed down, and that the coffin was not disturbed before they saw it put in the grave. Rowe said that on 10 November, at the parish workhouse, he identified the body taken from the kitchen at Millpleasant as Eliza's. Earlier he had been to her grave and seen that it had been disturbed. Some of the screws on the coffin had been removed, others, together with the garments with which the body had been clothed, were in the coffin, but not the body.

Jane Chapman said that she was present when Thomas Webb died. She and her sister-in-law, Grace Hamlyn, both testified that they had clothed the body in a linen shirt, a piece of cloth around the foot, a pair of white cotton stockings and a white cotton nightcap. They were present when the coffin was screwed down and had attended the burial, had seen the body at the workhouse on 10 November and had identified it as that of Thomas Webb. They identified the cotton stockings produced by the prosecution. Jane Chapman said that she went to the house at Millpleasant with Roger Halse on 11 November and there she found a pair of white cotton stockings in the under-cupboard in the bedroom. They were the same as those put on Mr Webb's body; there was a stain in one foot and they were marked "TB" at the top. She had received a piece of cloth from James Lancaster and had later given it to Grace Hamlyn. Grace Hamlyn confirmed having received it and that it was the cloth that she had put on Mr Webb's foot.

Elizabeth Brooks, wife of Thomas Brooks, a seaman of Stoke Damerel, said that Thomas Webb was her father. He died on 6 November. On the afternoon of Monday, the 8th, she saw his body in its coffin where it was fastened down and was with the coffin until she saw it put in its grave. The body was wearing, among other things, a pair of ribbed stockings with a blue rim round the tops and each was marked with the letters "TB". They had been marked by herself, had been mended and had belonged to her husband. She too confirmed that there was a wound in her father's foot around which a piece of calico had been wrapped before the sock was drawn over it.

Elizabeth Netting told the Court that Charity Netting had been her husband's mother and that she had known her well. She had died on 5th November and she, her daughter-in-law, had seen the body dressed in the clothes in which it was buried and had seen it put into the coffin and the coffin screwed down. It was taken almost at once to Stoke Damerel church and she had seen it put into the grave. The shift which James Day had found at 4 Millpleasant was shown to her and she identified it as the one in which Charity Netting had been buried. She refuted Louisa Goslin's claim to ownership of the shift. The dead woman had worn it during her lifetime and Elizabeth recognised it as her mother-in-law's work because the deceased had sewn left-handed. She confirmed that it was her husband's property.

The prosecution then produced evidence that Thomas Webb's coffin had still contained his grave clothes except his stockings; and that his body when found in Goslin's kitchen was dirty from the filthy sack in which it had been placed, while the stockings were perfectly clean, indicating that they had been taken from the body before it was put into the sack which, it was contended, proved deliberate intent to steal them.

The defence counsel, Mr Tonkin, accused the prosecution of bringing the cases of stealing the stockings and shift purely to increase the punishment which could be inflicted and maintained that the prisoners had only meant to steal the bodies, not the clothes. He further argued that no case could be proved against Mary Thompson and Louisa Goslin as there was no evidence that they had been present at the grave-robbing, and it was a principle of law that a woman committing a felony was under the power and authority of her husband and under his immediate control; therefore she had not sufficient power over her actions to be rendered liable for punishment. The women had been bound to receive their husbands when they returned home and, therefore, could not be considered accessories after the fact.

The prosecutor admitted that the point caused him to have doubts as to whether he had it in his power to prove the felony offence against the two women but, in response, brought in evidence to show that the defendants made a regular trade in the clothes as well as the bodies, and that Louisa Goslin had tried on the shift after it had been taken off the corpse.

While the jury considered the verdicts the 4 foot 11 inch, well-dressed Louisa Goslin, good-looking with a fair complexion, large grey eyes, a tip-tilted nose, and soft brown hair, stepped forward and addressed them. She said she had been thirty years in the world and had never been charged with a felony before. "Gentlemen of the jury", exclaimed Louisa, "it must have been either Thompson or Jones that brought the stockings into the house". That proved too much for Jones who roared out, "How could you say it's me what brought them into the house! I say it was Mr Goslin himself that brought them into the house and I get disgraced through you and Mr Goslin both. It's a hard case for me to be here for what I am innocent of". During the trial, as at the earlier Magistrates' Court hearing, those in Court, particularly the newspaper reporters, were impressed by the respectable, even prosperous appearance of the defendants. It was noticed that Thomas Goslin wore a large brooch on his shirt and, on the collar of his obviously expensive black coat, a piece of blue ribbon said to denote that he was a freemason.

The Court then heard the case against Nicholas Wood.

Constables Ambrose Nosworthy and Roger Halse told the Court of interviews with Nicholas Wood in the lock-up room at the town hall on 12th and 18th November. Nosworthy had taken in a bible requested by the prisoner. On his entering the cell Wood had said, "How do you do, Mr Nosworthy. This is a bad job and I am sorry for it". Asked how long he had been acquainted with Goslin, Wood replied, "About a month". He admitted that he had several times had a drink with Goslin at Mr Herring's, and at Mr Parnell's at the Military Hospital Inn, and to having had five or six glasses of liquor at Goslin's house. Wood agreed that he had told Mrs Goslin that the grave was not half filled in and that he would leave a shovel on old man Webb's grave and a board on top of another grave, so that they could easily be found in the dark and as signs they could be dug up. He claimed he had been asked by Goslin to let him have some teeth from the churchyard but had replied, "For God's sake don't meddle with the bodies". He insisted that he had agreed to the graves being opened only for the taking of teeth and not bodies. When Nosworthy asked him if he knew how many bodies Goslin had taken from the churchyard, Wood hesitated two or three minutes before answering, "Five or six".

Asked whether any of the other grave-diggers had anything to do with the grave-robbing, he replied that they had all drunk together but none of the others was involved and he, Wood, was to blame and no-one else. He had been drawn into it by Goslin and hoped he would be forgiven.

Goslin had kept on teasing him for a long time before he consented to do anything, and would not let him rest but followed him from place to place at public houses. Wood agreed that he had been to Goslin's house and received as much as half a sovereign at a time and several times a shilling or two. Nosworthy concluded his evidence by saying that on

18 November Wood admitted having received from Goslin thirty shillings for teeth and had said that it was a melancholy job, that he was ruined and had lost a good situation through that villain Goslin who had drawn him into it.

George Parnell, who kept the Military Hospital Inn in Stoke Damerel, confirmed that its location was about one hundred yards from the churchyard. He told the Court that he had known Wood over a period of years and had frequently seen him drinking with Thomas Goslin "and a woman who calls herself Louisa Goslin" in his public house. He said the Goslins sometimes remained together in the pub but Wood did not stay longer than a quarter of an hour at any one time. He had never seen the Goslins in his public house without seeing Wood come in while they were there. He testified that, in the last six weeks or two months, the three of them had been in the Military Hospital Inn at the same time and had drunk together but Wood had never paid for anything.

Another witness, Henry Lavis, gave evidence that he had seen Wood go to the house at 4 Millpleasant a number of times over a six week period and that, on one occasion, Wood told him that he had lent the people in that house a shovel to do up their garden.

Verdicts of "guilty" were brought in against both Goslins, Jones and Richard Thompson in connection with grave-robbing but Mary Thompson was acquitted. The same verdicts were returned in respect of stealing the grave clothes.

Because there was no evidence that the women had taken part in the actual robbing of the graves, and because women were held not to have sufficient wits to act on their own initiative and thus must act under the direction of their husbands, Mary Thompson was acquitted of both offences. Louisa Goslin too could have escaped punishment had she not insisted that she had taken part in grave-robbing and would do so again, and had it not been proved that she had traded in grave-clothes and actually tried on the shift.

Nicholas Wood was found "guilty as charged".

The Sessions Order Book records, for the Goslins, Richard Thompson and Jones:

For the misdemeanour, i.e., stealing the bodies, "Let them be imprisoned in Bridewell for a fortnight". For the felony, i.e., stealing the stockings and the shift, "Severally convicted of larceny. Let them be transported to such parts beyond the seas as His Majesty shall appoint for the term of seven years."

For Nicholas Wood:-

"Guilty of misdemeanour. To be imprisoned in Bridewell for twelve months."

For Mary Thompson:-

"Acquitted of misdemeanour. Let her be discharged.

Thomas Goslin's response to the sentence was to ask the Court to compel Richard Ellis to hand back to him the human teeth which had been taken from his house as he wished to sell them and make money of them. His application was refused.

Goslin may have made the application out of impudence or bravado, but it could have been because he knew only too well what lay ahead of them, and remembered from his past imprisonments that, with an amount of cash in his possession, he might be able to make life a little easier for himself and Louisa "beyond the seas". He repeatedly claimed that the house at 4 Millpleasant and its contents belonged to him. It is not known whether that was true and, if so, whether he was able to have them converted into cash.

CHAPTER TWELVE

The Mystery

It is a mystery why, at Stoke Damerel, Thomas Vaughan committed the crime he had taken such care to avoid during his previous thirteen years robbing graves. That he was aware of the pitfall is clear from his reply to the Union Hall Officers when they arrested him in 1828: "Clarke, you ought to know me better than that. If I have taken the body, they will find the gown, no doubt of it, at the foot of the coffin". What happened to change his practice in the two years between 1828 and 1830?

During the time that Vaughan was incarcerated for the Great Yarmouth offences, Sir Astley Cooper paid six shillings "to Vaughan's wife". There is nothing to say that the "wife" was Louisa. It may or may not have been, given the irregular lifestyle of the rest of the gang. No record of a marriage between Vaughan and Louisa has been found. If he was legally married, according to Bransby Cooper's account, he was not averse to making overtures to other young women at Great Yarmouth and Stoke Damerel.

At the trial for the Stoke Damerel offences it was said that the defendants had made a regular trade in grave clothes; presumably sold as "second-hand". Given that it had always been second nature to Vaughan to avoid stealing anything other than the body because of the severe penalty that such theft carried, it points to one of the others being the culprit. Louisa would most likely have been the principal. Had it not been Louisa it is extremely unlikely that a man as canny as Vaughan would have allowed himself to become implicated in it. Why did not or could not he dissuade her from the trade? Was she greedy for money, headstrong or was he so besotted that he could refuse her nothing? It is hard to imagine a man of Vaughan's character and habits being in love with anyone.

What of Louisa's character? At some time she had worked as a plain cook. She did not mind being seen drinking in public houses, a thing no respectable woman would do. On the convict transport to Van Diemen's Land she did well as a teacher. She was good-looking and well-dressed, yet a woman who could try on a garment taken straight off a stolen corpse. She admitted taking part in grave-robbing and showed no remorse. In effect she appears to have sought the punishment of gaol and transportation which she might have avoided. Did she do it to be with her husband? Many wives of transported convicts joined their husbands by buying passage on a ship bound for Australia or Van Diemen's Land and becoming "free settlers". At the time of the 1830 trial

Albemarle Villas, Stoke Damerel c.1820. The genteel community as the grave-robbers would have seen it.

the Vaughans were not, by their accounts, short of money. As a plain cook she could have found employment, supported herself and stayed in England. She would not have been destitute without a husband to support her. Or she could have supervised the sale of their furniture, and the house if they owned it, and taken the money to fund their time in Van Diemen's Land. Did she decide to implicate herself and share her husband's punishment from feelings of guilt? She would have known that Vaughan had steered clear of stealing grave clothes for the whole of his criminal career. Had he not taken clothes from the Stoke Damerel graves he could have continued his lucrative trade of robbing graves, with only the inconvenience of minor punishments.

Perhaps, against all the odds, there was a love story here.

CHAPTER THIRTEEN

Aftermath at Stoke Damerel

T he revelations of such appalling body trade activities certainly took a toll on the parish of Stoke Damerel. For some time relatives and friends of the deceased kept watch by the gravesides as the notoriety of the churchyard grew. A bird-catcher, described as a "poor fellow", was dared by some dockyard apprentices to go into the churchyard at midnight. His spirits bolstered by strong drink, he bravely entered it only to be pounced on by the watch and brought before the magistrates on suspicion of being a grave-robber. However, they believed his story and let him go. Stories about the 1830 grave-robbers abound and over the generations these stories have become embroidered in the community. An amusing embellishment is a story still repeated today. It goes:-

Grave-robbing being suspected, a peace officer kept watch on the churchyard one dark night. A pony and trap came towards him in the darkness and stopped close by. He watched as the driver descended and, together with the passenger in the back of the trap, went off carrying spades, ropes and other tools. The watching officer heard the sounds of earth being shovelled and soon one of the men returned carrying a large bundle over his shoulder. He pushed and pulled the bundle into the front seat beside the driver's position, took an overcoat from the back of the trap and wrapped it around the bundle and put a hat on top. When the man went off to join his companion somewhere in the darkness, the officer emerged from his hiding place and examined the bundle, which he found to be a corpse. He placed the corpse out of sight behind vault, put the overcoat around his own shoulder, the hat on his head, and took the place of the corpse in the front of the trap, prepared to travel with them to their lair and expose the villains. Eventually the robbers returned, loaded their tools into the trap and climbed aboard. As they drove off the driver commented aloud that it was a cold night. "It is", replied the unthinking "corpse", to the horror and astonishment of the criminals, who are said to have run away in fright, only to be apprehended later.

Another tale has the gang operating in a churchyard in the nearby Stonehouse and ending up fatally trapped inside a vault by its heavy lid.

The old saying has it that it is an ill-wind that blows nobody good, and so it was with the grave-robbings in Stoke Damerel churchyard. For some years medical men throughout the country had petitioned Parliament to legalise dissection and the supply of bodies for the study of anatomical science. The local medical society later supplied details of the activities in Stoke Damerel churchyard of Goslin and his gang to Thomas Wakely, a Member of Parliament for

The church of Stoke Damerel as it is today. The area retains a melancholic air.

Finsbury, who was a well-known medical reformer and the first editor of the *Lancet*. Wakely, who was himself a surgeon and a coroner, gave evidence on the subject before a commission set up to investigate grave-robbing; of which more later.

Over thirty years later, in 1870, Her Majesty's Inspector of Graveyards received a letter telling him that a Government Order of 1862 restricting the use of Stoke Damerel churchyard for burials was being ignored. It alleged the churchyard was overcrowded and had been so for years and that a dreadful smell was now arising from it. With a party of officials that included the Mayor of Devonport, Mr May; the Principal Medical Officer in charge of the Royal Military Hospital opposite the church, Dr Gallway; and the Registrar, Mr Rickard, the Inspector visited the church-yard to be met by the Rector, the Rev. W.J. St Aubyn ("the bad St Aubyn") and his curates, Rev. J. Clarke and Rev. R. Lemon.

Before the Inspector could begin the Inquiry he had to deal with an outburst from the Rector who accused one of his curates, Mr Clarke, of writing the "meddling and interfering" letter of complaint. The Inspector said he had been asked by the informant not to divulge his name and none of the statements contained in the letter would have any effect upon his report unless they were substantiated. After a stand-off the curate finally admitted to having written the letter but said he had not asked the Inspector to conceal his name but the name of the real complainant. The Rector called him a "blackguard" and said the churchyard was not overcrowded and no smell arose from it; if there was a smell it did not come from the churchyard but from the Royal Military Hospital opposite. The Principal Medical Officer was not having that. He said there was no smell arising from the Royal Military Hospital; if it did not come from the churchyard then it came from the creek beside which both places stood and into which the sewers of Devonport emptied. The Mayor of Devonport defended the Borough's sewage system but eventually the Inspector was able to get the Inquiry underway by calling the Sexton. He said that when he was required to open a vault, he and his men tied handkerchiefs over their noses and mouths while they lifted the lid, then they ran off until the odour has dispersed. He said that when he was required to dig a new grave he took a long spear and went around probing the ground. If the spear went into the ground without hitting anything that was where he dug a grave. Or if he found a little space near a coffin he dug the grave to cram another coffin in beside it. The curate, Mr Clarke, said he had been conducting a burial in the eastern churchyard when the combined weight of the mourners at the graveside squeezed out from beneath their feet a skeleton which shot out sideways and dropped down onto the newly lowered coffin.

The Principal Medical Officer declared that if the statements made were true, then the churchyard was a health hazard. The Rector said the churchyard has been in existence long before it was decided to build a hospital and he called to the Registrar to confirm there was less mortality

Gravestones in St Andrew's churchyard Stoke Damerel.

in the nearby area than in other parts of Stoke. The Registrar confirmed the Rector's point but said they did not need to wait until someone was killed before acting.

The Rector tried by every means to get an Order for the churchyard to remain open and offered to give all kinds of undertakings to make this possible. The Inspector pointed out, amid the laughter of the others, that all the undertakings he had given in the past he had failed to keep. The curate, Mr Clarke, said the Inspector would not have returned to London a fortnight before he would be forced to come down again because the Order would be infringed. Stung, the Rector retorted that there was nothing Mr Clarke would not do to annoy him. Mr Clarke thereupon took his last shot at the Rector by saying to the Inspector, "If the Government makes an Order to close this churchyard, I trust the Rector will restore to the churchyard the headstones that he has taken from it to pave the floors of his greenhouse and kitchen house at the Rectory".

The churchyard was closed in 1871 by an Order from Her Majesty's Privy Council and has not been used for burials since then.

CHAPTER FOURTEEN

Transportation

As punishment for crime, transportation has a long history in England. The English Parliament enacted the first direct law associated with transportation in 1598. Convicted villains were to be "banished out of this realm… and conveyed unto such perils beyond the seas as shall be at any time hereafter assigned for the purpose by the Privy Council". Those found guilty of the crimes of robbery and felony were ordered by Council in 1615 to be used for service in the West Indies or American plantations.

During the 18th century transportation became even more common and, by the 19th, colonisation of Australia saw thousands sent from both county gaols and prison hulks to New South Wales and Van Diemen's Land.

Following a convict's sentencing to transportation, he was first sent to a gaol or hulk to await the execution of the sentence. Hulks were dismasted ships used as prisons and were an integral part of the convict system in England and Australia. They were entirely mobile and provided an excellent workforce. The convicts ate and slept on the hulk, but by day worked on the land in gangs under strict supervision. When the hulks were full to their establishment for convicted men, a ship was commissioned to take those sentenced to transportation overseas. Women were not sent to hulks but kept in prison until a sufficient number were awaiting transportation to make it worth the Government's while to charter a ship to take them overseas.

The River Tamar, which forms a boundary between Devon and Cornwall, reaches the sea in Plymouth Sound. Where the river flows between Torpoint, on the Cornwall side, and Devonport it is called the Hamoaze. Since the 18th century the land on the Devonport side has been mainly covered by the naval dockyard.

When the fourteen days imprisonment with hard labour had been served at Exeter Bridewell Louisa was taken to another prison. It was to the hulk appropriately named *Captivity*, anchored in the Hamoaze, that Thomas Goslin, John Jones and Richard Thompson (for the only time on record, with the alias Mann) were sent when they had served their sentences of two weeks in the Bridewell for the grave-robbing. While awaiting the transportation ship, convicts on the *Captivity* were made to labour in Devonport dockyard. In 1830 four hundred convicts were on board and worked in various departments of the dockyard. Goslin, Thompson and Jones were not sent to work as labourers but kept on the hulk. It would seem local opinion was still violently against them and the authorities feared that if they were put on shore they might be killed so they lived and worked on *Captivity*.

The harbour at Devonport showing the Captivity, *formerly HMS* Bellerophon, *c.1829.*

The hulk return for January-June 1831 records:-

Prisoner: Richard Thompson alias Mann. Age 24.
  Offence: Disinterring 2 dead bodies and stealing grave clothes.
  Convicted: Exeter. When Sentenced: 7 December 1830
  Sentence: 7 years.
Prisoner: Thomas Goslin alias Vaughan. Age 39.
  Offence: Disinterring 2 dead bodies and stealing grave clothes.
  Convicted: Exeter. When Sentenced: 7 December 1830
  Sentence: 7 years.
Prisoner: John Jones alias Quinn. Age 27.
  Offence: Disinterring 2 dead bodies and stealing grave clothes.
  Convicted: Exeter. When Sentenced: 7 December 1830
  Sentence: 7 years.

No comments were shown under the headings "Bodily State" and "Behaviour". An earlier hulk return for December 1830 showed the men as above but, under "Bodily Health", all had "Good"; there were no comments under the "Behaviour" heading.

The hulk *Captivity* had seen stirring days. It had started life as a 74 gun warship; the first of the "seventy-fours". Weighing 1,613 tons with a length of 168 feet, breadth of 46 feet 10 inches and 19 feet 9inches depth of hull, the ship had been launched in 1786 and named *Bellerophon*. She carried a crew of 590 men and made her reputation in the twenty years war against the French and Napoleon Bonaparte. The ship came to be known affectionately as the "Billy Ruffian".

Bonaparte had surrendered to the Allies on board *Bellerophon* and he was quartered on the ship in Plymouth Sound until it was decided that he should be taken into exile. Every day he took his exercise on the deck, and every day hundreds of small boats crammed with sightseers rowed out to *Bellerophon*, while it was anchored in Plymouth Sound, in the hope of catching a glimpse of the man whose name had struck terror in their hearts for so many years, and was still used to frighten naughty children.

NOTICE.

PRISONERS admitted into Pentonville Prison will have an opportunity of being taught a Trade, and of receiving sound Moral and Religious Instruction. They will be transported to a Penal Colony, in Classes, as follows:—

FIRST CLASS.

Prisoners who shall, when sent from this Prison, be reported by the Governor and Chaplain to have behaved well.

These, at the end of 18 months, will be sent to Van Diemen's Land, to receive a Ticket of Leave, on landing, which, until forfeited by bad conduct, will, in that Country, confer most of the advantages of freedom. In Van Diemen's Land, labor being in great demand, and wages being therefore high, the Prisoner's knowledge of a trade, and the possession of a Ticket of Leave, will enable him, with industry and continued good conduct, to secure a comfortable and respectable position in Society. Prisoners who obtain Tickets of Leave may also, by industry and good conduct, acquire, in a short time, means sufficient to enable their families to follow them.

SECOND CLASS.

Prisoners who have not behaved well.

These, also, at the end of 18 months, will be transported to Van Diemen's Land where they will receive a Probationary Pass, which will secure to them only a limited portion of their earnings, will admit of their enjoying only a small portion of liberty, and will subject them to many restraints and privations.

THIRD CLASS.

Prisoners who have behaved ill.

These will be transported to Tasman's Peninsula, a Penal Colony, occupied only by Convicts and the Military Guard, there to be employed on the Public Works, in Probationary Gangs, without wages, and deprived of liberty; and their families will not be permitted, under any circumstances, to follow them.

Prisoners will see how much depends on their own conduct during their confinement in this Prison. According to their behaviour and improvement here, will be their future condition in the Colony to which they will be sent.

A notice issued to prisoners who were to be transported.

When *Bellerophon* ceased to be a fighting ship and became a hulk, at first it kept its proud name but in 1826 it was changed to *Captivity*. The ship continued as a hulk until 1836 when it was sold to a ship breaker.

Life on board *Captivity* was described by another John Jones, a fourteen-year old convict sent to it from the Cornwall Assize Court in March 1829:- "I was removed from Bodmin 14 days after my trial, and sent to Plymouth, and stationed in the dockyard gang drawing timber about from place to place, shifting manure, and emptying cesspools; in fact all the heavy work the labourers refused to do, the convicts are compelled to do. The most dreadful punishments the convicts are subject to for offences on board the hulks are various; they have to work in double irons on board the hulks; I was placed in heavy irons but being young, was greatly favoured by one of the keepers. The treatment the convicts received on board the hulks is tolerably good to what it is abroad. I thought after having lived with my parents in Camborne that the hulks were very miserable. Imagine, my friends, a boy (a mere infant you may say) bound with great chains around my poor body and legs".

Of his voyage to Van Diemen's Land young Jones recounted: "The ship taking our troops we received many comforts we should not have had, being in some measure situated as they were, but with this difference – that we were chained fifteen on each side of the deck by day, at night stoved into a little crib, with scarcely sufficient room to turn, still having our irons on, but those who go in regular convict ships do not receive such kind treatment as we did; they would be bound together similar to the manner in which pigs are brought from Ireland to England – they are placed on each side of the ship, chained to each other, similar to oxen in a yoke. There is no punishment on board ship for committing a crime, nothing more than a good lashing from the keepers to keep them in good order, or extra weight of irons. And is not this enough to deter a man from committing a crime? If the convict next to you has any spite against you, he has nothing to do but rattle his chains and make a noise, or push you when a keeper is looking at you, when a cane would be used pretty smartly across your back; and if you murmured in the least, a report was made to the captain, who if he is like the greater part of the men in charge of these vessels, takes down every report against you, and these are handed over to the authorities on landing (the crimes some are transported for will not commit them to the chain gang) but the reports of the captain are against the party, who at the earliest opportunity are sent to the Penal Settlement".

The four grave-robbers were transported to Van Diemen's Land. They had to endure a long sea voyage to a destination at the bottom of the world in cramped unpleasant conditions rendered worse by the heat of the tropics, with the vessel at the mercy of wind and waves. The three men sailed on the convict transport *Argyle* and Louisa on the female convict ship *Mary*.

When Captain James Cook made his second voyage of discovery to Australia, in 1772 in command of HMS *Resolution*, he was accompanied the son of a Stoke Damerel land-owning family, Captain Tobias Furneaux in command of HMS *Adventure*. When a young naval second lieutenant, Tobias Furneaux sailed with Captain Wallis in HMS *Dolphin* to explore for the unknown lands believed to lie in the Southern hemisphere and Tobias Furneaux became the first white man to step on Tahiti when, with the Captain of *Dolphin* ill, he was given command of a boat which put ashore to get water and food. He circumnavigated the globe West to East in *Dolphin* and East to West in *Adventure*, becoming the first man to circumnavigate the globe in both directions. When he sailed to accompany Captain Cook, while Captain Cook mapped the coast of Australia, he sent Captain Furneaux to explore and chart the island of Tasmania. Captain Furneaux named several places on the coast after his home area; Eddystone Point, Mewstone, and Swilly Bay. When Captain Cook discovered a group of islands to the north-east of Tasmania he named them after his friend, the Furneaux islands.

It is ironic that when he was charting Tasmania, there was no way Captain Furneaux could foresee that the island would become a penal

Captain Tobias Furneaux's memorial at Stoke Damerel church.

colony, and that among the prisoners held there would be four who were there for robbing the churchyard where Captain Furneaux himself and generations of his ancestors were buried. Captain Furneaux's grave lies near the north door of Stoke Damerel church; and the last member of the Furneaux family to worship in the church died in 1996.

CHAPTER FIFTEEN

The Misery of the Voyages

On completion of a contract for the transportation of a shipload, generally from 200 to 300 convicts, they were put on board under the control of a Surgeon Superintendent. He was then responsible for their health and safe delivery to the administrator of the penal colonies in New South Wales or Van Diemen's Land. The ships always carried a detachment of soldiers who were often accompanied by their wives and children. The voyage usually took three months. The surgeon's log records the voyage of each of the convict ships which, altogether, carried over 150,000 convicts to the penal colonies until the practice ceased in 1853.

The *Argyle* embarked 250 convicts, the greater part of whom were taken from the prison hulks at Portsmouth on 15 February 1831, and the remainder from *Captivity* on the Hamoaze at Devonport some nine days later. Henry Brock, the surgeon superintendent on the *Argyle* made these comments in his log during the voyage of some 138 days to Van Diemen's Land. "We received our Sailing orders on 7th March, however the ship was detained at Plymouth until 18th March when sails were set and the voyage to Van Diemen's Land commenced. The winter had been harsh and both previous and subsequent to the departure there was encountered a succession of cold, wet and stormy weather."

Mr Brock, a seasoned surgeon on convict transports, attributed the early appearance of sickness on board to these extreme conditions. At first it was confined to the convicts but subsequently affected many of the guard and some of the sailors. In addition to the prevalence of this bad weather that seemed never to let up, the surgeon also noted in his journal that this had been a major reason for the rigid confinement under which it was found necessary to keep the convicts during the greater part of the voyage. Another reason had been a conspiracy in which a number of convicts had unsuccessfully tried to capture the ship, for which crime twelve of the ring leaders were tried and found guilty. On arrival these men were to be sent to the penal settlement at Macquarie Harbour.

The voyage had been marked by continuous fever among those on board so that, by 3 May, the surgeon's store of treatments for this ailment had run out. As it was essential that the medicines be replaced, the ship had to make an unscheduled visit to Rio de Janiero to take on a full supply of treatments. During the voyage over 60 pe cent of the prisoners were ill.

Louisa did not set sail until 8 June 1831 in the female convict transport *Mary*, which sailed from Woolwich with 151 female prisoners and their children. The convicts' health was good. They had all been checked and found to be free of infections.

Long and arduous voyages lasting from 90 to 120 days meant that those on board were deprived of fresh food. Children and women were particularly likely to suffer from scurvy in those conditions. There was also a tendency for convict ships to avoid restocking with fresh supplies during the voyage, as their masters were extremely anxious to deliver their cargo as quickly as possible. The *Mary* was fortunate to have a good surgeon, Samuel Sinclair MD, whose stores prepared him well to combat sea scurvy, and whose hygiene procedures prevented many illnesses. He was concerned with the fact that some of these female prisoners had been in English county gaols for periods up to three years on a poor diet which at times had consisted solely of bread and water. The confinement on board ship did little to improve their constitutions.

In severe weather swing stoves were kept alight to preserve warmth for the prisoners and as an aid to drying their drenched quarters. The *Mary* was a "flush ship" and unluckily shipped a lot of water in rough weather. It was during such times when the decks were constantly wet and when heat and dryness were most required, that the stoves could not be used with safety to the ship, or to the women employed at them as, due to the rolling and pitching motions of the ship, they could not stand to attend to them.

All the prisoners on the *Mary* were subject to two washing days each week, when an allowance of soap and fresh water heated in a copper was supplied to them. Their clothes were hung on deck on make-shift clothes lines. The matrons of each convict class were responsible for any further washing being done in the prison or the hospital. It was strictly forbidden for any wet linen or clothing to be hung up to dry below decks. The women were kept employed as much as possible throughout the day in their respective classes by constant work that included teaching each other, for which purpose three schools were established.

It was at teaching that Louisa Goslin was found to be most proficient. The surgeon remarked in his final report on her conduct that she had been an excellent schoolmistress. For these services she was duly rewarded and paid a pound a day. In a time when a skilled man only earned thirty shillings a week, this was a generous amount. By the end of the voyage she had earned £100 which the surgeon superintendent held on her behalf. On arrival in Van Diemen's Land the surgeon superintendent would have deposited the money in the Derwent Bank. Unfortunately the records of the Derwent Bank are not available so it is not possible to check whether Louisa was able to keep the money in her own name, as a nest egg. Equally it is not possible to check whether she and Thomas had money transferred there from England from, say, the sale of the Millpleasant house.

To keep the women and children as healthy as possible the surgeon maintained a reasonable diet and organised exercises on the deck in fine weather. There was dancing in the evenings for an hour to promote good circulation. The conditions on board made it difficult to keep the passengers healthy, particularly in poor weather. Louisa was not once mentioned on the surgeon's sick list during the 16,000 mile voyage. When she arrived in Van Diemen's Land she had lost an upper tooth and had three scars on the right side of her face, which had not been remarked upon by the reporters at her trial.

The majority of prisoners slept three to a bed and the moral conduct was, the surgeon wrote, " best left to one's own imagination". Although strict moral conduct was encouraged, along with strict attention to religious instruction during the voyage, what went on below decks was in some cases unimaginable.

CHAPTER SIXTEEN

Servitude in Van Diemen's Land

Named after Anthony Van Diemen, Governor of Batavia, Van Diemen's Land is an island not quite the size of Ireland. It lies south of mainland Australia. It became a self-governing colony of the British under Colonel George Arthur. It was first discovered in 1642 by a Dutch navigator, Abel Tasman, after whom it was later renamed, Tasmania. The first European immigrants were convicts and their gaolers who settled first at Risdon's Cove, and later at Sullivan's Cove, now Hobart.

No colony could have begun under worse circumstances. Every kind of irregularity, debauchery and vice was practised. Both officers and prisoners lived in moral anarchy, and it was not until the second decade of the nineteenth century that free settlers arrived who, with their descendants, were to dominate and shape society for the rest of the century.

The sight that met the eyes of the convicts on board *Argyle* was not reassuring as the ship approached the coast and landfall. One author describes the sighting of the coast in the 1830s and the passage into the Derwent river before anchoring at Hobart:

The first glance of its coast is harsh and unattractive. The landfall usually made is either the south or south-west cape, and as these are without inhabitants, the air of the region is chill, desolate and barren; the rugged cliff and primeval forest extend in unbroken solitude for many miles.

The Lieutenant Governor General of Van Diemen's Land was a Plymouth man. He had been born in Norley House and when he grew up he joined the Army where he rose rapidly through the ranks. He had no patron. His rapid promotion was due to his great bravery, sound judgement and common sense. He received the Freedom of the City of London in recognition of his bravery and later he received the Freedom of

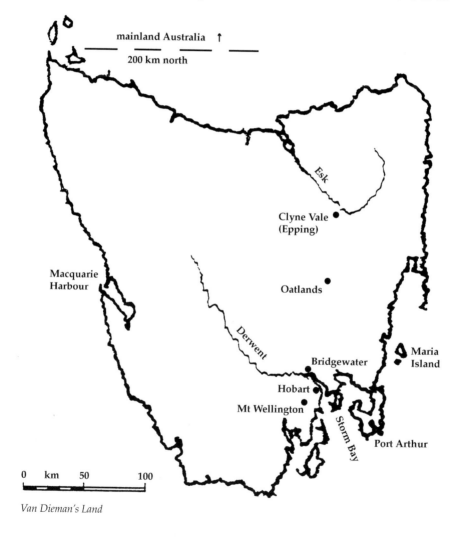

Van Dieman's Land

Plymouth. When he became Lieutenant Governor he instituted a system of assignment whereby the convicts were put to work for either the government or the free settlers. With it he had a reward and punishment system. Free settlers who chose to live in what was essentially a colonial prison and were prepared to conform to its regulations, were rewarded and aided in their efforts to accumulate wealth by being given assigned servants (convicts) to work on the land and in the businesses in the towns. Failure to comply with the Governor's rules resulted in assigned servants being withdrawn. As convicts were the only source of labour, settlers were unable to operate their farms or businesses without them. Under the same system convicts were rewarded for good behaviour and punished for bad. There was an elaborate system of prisoner classification which allowed for the most favoured ticket-of-leave men and women to work as virtually free while the worst were held in chains at Port Arthur. Colonel Arthur controlled all manner of things, including confirmation of sentences imposed by magistrates, the granting of all tickets-of-leave and requests for permission to marry.

The assignment system was open to abuse. Convict women who were assigned to work as servants lived in a world outside the prison; however their lives were completely dominated by their masters, lack of money, lack of clothing, and the conditions imposed on them by the law. During the voyage to the penal colony they had been sexually vulnerable to the ship's crew. There was little chance of the authorities protecting them. When assigned to work as servants they were at the mercy of their master if he chose to take advantage of them sexually or assault them. Their plight was made worse by the belief that a female convict must be a "bad woman" as opposed to a "good woman", which led to the assumption that she must therefore be a prostitute. Although convict women generally had been bad characters most were not prostitutes. However to escape the hard conditions assignment brought them, women sought refuge among other convict women in the brothels of Hobart town, where they could earn a little money and develop an extended social life.

For middle and upper class gentlemen in the nineteenth century "good women" were the wives, mothers, sisters and daughters who were safely under their control. Working class women seemed to be the opposite; they often appeared to be outside the control of men; they worked outside the home, which was the proper sphere of women; they seemed to wander the streets freely and were often poorly or immodestly dressed and rowdy in their behaviour, and sometimes they drank. The term "prostitute" was used broadly in those days to condemn a woman's behaviour as well as to describe her profession. A woman might be described as a prostitute if she lived in a *de facto* relationship, shared a house with another woman or was out in the street at night without a male family member as escort. Most of those transported gave as their profession ordinary working class occupations, such as seamstress, domestic servant, children's nurse and factory hand. A typical woman convict was likely to be transported for seven years for the kind of petty theft which is driven by need, if she had a record of similar minor crimes and was in her twenties or younger and was single. The moral standards of male convicts were not a matter of any comment unless they were suspected of homosexuality.

When *Argyle,* and indeed all convict transports, arrived the prisoners were all assembled on deck and examined, along with the state of the ship, by the Port Officer, the Colonial Secretary and the Colonial Surgeon. The last also received the report of the ship's surgeon on the health and conduct of the prisoners during the voyage. The Lieutenant Governor then came on board and addressed the convicts, after which they were marched from the ship to the gaol. The muster master interviewed and made a record of each convict. He examined them minutely regarding their past life, crimes, marks of identification and details such as age. In due course the records included details of later events in the convict's life. These records can be seen in the Tasmanian archives in Hobart.

Any money the convicts had with them was taken and put into a savings bank. Each convict was then given a police number, along with the name of the ship that had brought him, as his identification. Thomas Goslin's number was 756 *Argyle*.

In his "Horrors of Transportation" the other, 14 year old, John Jones said that male convicts "… were dressed in grey- and yellow-striped clothing, the yellow stripes leading from the shoulders to the leg, the waistcoat has one yellow and one grey side to it. Females here wear no irons – their dress is a green bedgown, with a red petticoat, and a white cap with no border; their hair is kept very close under their caps, and for punishment they will have it cut. But those females for life wear a yellow bedgown with great petticoat; but if the females offer to disobey against any of those rules that are laid down before them, then they are punished severely. They are placed in what they call the washing gang – washing the coarse clothing of their fellow convicts, chained from six o'clock in the morning till six at night to a washing tray: while others are carrying a heavy burden to a considerable distance: but if they offer to disobey against those hardened drivers, they are taken from their horrible work, and brought to a dungeon, confined in heavy irons till they are nearly starved to death, or subjected to some other dreadful punishment. But we must confess, that if a female is inclined to do good for herself, she has many opportunities afforded her of doing so. Almost immediately upon arriving at the Island, they are hired out as servants by mistresses and masters, and very soon after gain their freedom upon the Island."

Thomas Goslin's ship record was good. As he could read and write well, he was assigned as a constable. There were constables of various grades selected from the free settlers and ticket-of-leave men. When Governor Arthur took over the colony he found "the whole class of petty constables were convicts who were more given to committing than detecting crime".

On 2 February 1832 Goslin was fined for improperly being on the premises of a Mr A Wrighte and for insolence. In May that year he was fined ten shillings for being drunk. A further offence of being drunk in September led to him being suspended for one month. On 21 January

1833 he was sentenced to be imprisoned for three months with hard labour, for misconduct in receiving a bribe, and was dismissed from his office of constable. A few days later, for neglect of duty while in the chain gang, he was given twenty lashes. On 8 February, again for neglect of duty, he received a sentence of imprisonment with hard labour, in addition to the sentence he was already serving. On 5 March, for refusing to work the previous day while in a road party, he was placed on short rations for a week.

His record remains clear of further trouble until 11 February 1834 when, acting as a constable for a settler, Captain James Crear, "improper conduct" led to him being dismissed as a constable and reassigned to work for the government.

Captain Crear RN had been the master of the ship *Triton* and had arrived in Van Diemen's Land from Leith, Scotland, in 1824 when he received his original land grant of some 700 acres fronting the river Esk. The property was named Clyne Vale after his wife's maiden name. He left the property in the care of a neighbour and in 1828 a brick house was built ready for the Crear family's migration and arrival in 1831.

Assigned servants at Clyne Vale occupied quarters in the woolshed which was distinguished by a prominent ecclesiastical end window. Thomas and Louisa may have been famliar with this building as each was assigned to Captain Crear for a period in 1834. On 24 April 1834 Goslin was charged with "gross insolence to Master Crear and using improper language reflecting on his late master, J Crear, Esq". He was sentenced to be imprisoned and kept to hard labour for six months, and the Bridgewater chain gang was recommended as his destination.

The system of assigning some convicts to settlers and others for public works, was paramount for the development of the colony, particularly in the building of main roads through the interior, the making of streets in towns and the construction of bridges. This was perhaps the most labour intensive activity during Governor Arthur's administration of the colony.

The penal station at Bridgewater served as a repository for those convicts engaged in the building of a causeway across the Derwent river. Quarrying of the stone was done only a short distance away. G.T.W.B. Boyes, Colonial Auditor, when visiting the station in 1831 with a surgeon, recorded that "these men were in a situation which, to men not entirely callous to bodily suffering nor lost to a sense of human degradation, must have been one of exquisite moral and physical misery". Things had not changed very much when Goslin arrived.

In her book *Ship Thieves*, Sian Reeves describes life in a chain gang: "Locked in huts so small that the whole number could neither stand upright nor sit down at the same time except with their legs at right angles to their bodies and which in some instances do not allow more than 18 inches in width for each individual to lie down upon bare boards. At 5.30 a.m. called to muster and marched to quarries. After three hours given a pint of skilly (a hasty pudding composed of flour, water and salt). Lunch was mutton and potatoes and if an overseer fancied a man's bowl for himself or his favourite, that man was wise to say nothing. Watched by soldier guards, each convict wore the hated iron bar between his legs and slops patched with blue and yellow; each was chained to the next. When they returned to camp at the end of the day more skilly was sent to the cells and the prisoners were bolted in, left caged and unattended. What happened at night was degraded and incorrigible."

Life in the chain-gang left Goslin uncrushed. A year later he received twenty-five lashes for disobedience of orders and making use of threatening language. On 9th January 1837 he was sentenced to three months hard labour for being out after hours and drunkenness. An entry in the records kept for convicts in servitude in the northern part of Van Diemen's Land shows him obtaining a ticket-of-leave on 21 July 1838, while a charge of assault on 29 July 1838 was dismissed.

Tickets-of-leave were a convict's first step towards a freer life. Applications had to be made to magistrates and required a convict to have been in employment and of good conduct. When granted, a ticket-of-leave allowed a convict to seek employment for a wage or to work in a business of his own. They were required to report to the magistrate at regular intervals, were not allowed to leave the district in which the ticket was granted and could not change their abode without permission of the magistrate and were required to attend church services. It was possible to apply for a ticket-of-leave after four years of the sentence of seven years' imprisonment.

When the *Mary* arrived in Hobart in October 1831 the muster master boarded the ship to take the details of this latest arrival of female convicts. As usual, Governor Arthur went aboard too to give his normal talk to the assembled convicts. He was a deeply religious man and proceeded with his explanation of salvation by announcing that the way to redemption was to have faith and that, by order, they were to attend church twice on each and every Sunday. Many examples of good and bad behaviour were also given, along with the prospect of an early ticket-of-leave as an incentive.

Louisa gave her age as thirty-one, occupation as a plain cook, and her place of birth as London. The surgeon of the *Mary* had used her talents well on the voyage, as her indent record states that her behaviour on board was exemplary and good, and that she had been an excellent schoolmistress to the convicts and their children during the passage from England. At the conclusion of her interrogation Louisa was given a police number *111 Mary* (the name of her ship) as her only means of identification for the next seven years. She was given an issue of new clothing and sent to the female prison to await her first assignment.

Almost immediately she was assigned to a Mr Horne, most probably the barrister, Thomas Horne, whose residence was in Collin Street, Hobart. Only weeks after her arrival she was sentenced to the crime class of the house of correction for "turning the tap of a beer barrel with a fork for the purpose of drawing off beer without permission and afterwards locking the store room door whereby the beer was floating over the room". Two and a half years then passed without a recorded incident.

There is every possibility that Louisa was able to meet Thomas shortly after her arrival and assignment as Thomas was at that time a constable in Hobart. His time in road gangs, imprisonment, the lash and hard labour would have parted them but his reinstatement as a constable to Captain Crear and her assignment to Clyne Vale would have re-united them for a time in 1834. When Thomas's "improper conduct" led to him being sent from Clyne Vale, Louisa's dissatisfaction or bitterness was evidenced by her own outbreak of disobedience. At the end of March 1834 she was given fourteen days' solitary confinement on bread and water for disobedience of Crear's orders.

In September 1834 insolence and improper conduct at Crear's earned her six months in the "female factory" at the Cascades in Hobart. Often women used certain offences, such as insolence, refusal to work, or absence for a short time, which carried small punishments, as a means of changing their place of service. Clyne Vale was a long way from Hobart and Thomas, and Louisa probably used this ploy to follow her husband.

The "female factory", as it was popularly called, was a maternity hospital for women convicts as well as a house of correction and a nursery. The building had formerly been a distillery. It was cold and damp, situated in a dark, dank valley about a mile and a half above Hobart.

In "the factory" the female convicts were divided into three classes. The first class was reserved for those women recently arrived from England who had had no complaints made about them during their voyage; women who had been returned from service with good characters, and women who had served a probationary period in the second class. When jobs were available all women in this class were eligible for assignment. The second class consisted of women who had been found guilty of minor offences, or warranted removal from the third class for good behaviour, or had served out a trouble-free probationary period of three months. The third class was reserved for those women who had been transported for a second time and had been found guilty of misconduct on their voyage or after their arrival. Louisa may have found herself in the first class as her indent record shows no entry for the six-month period September 1834 to March 1835.

During the mid-1830s there were many allegations with regard to the cleanliness of the institution, however, during a visit to "the factory" in October 1834, during Louisa's incarceration, the prisoners were all found to be very clean but the overcrowding was described as unbelievable. Over twenty adults and forty-two babies were crammed into two rooms of which the combined size was only 45 x 11 feet. A prisoner and overseer of the children, Elizabeth Flint, stated that in one room with seven beds, seven women and thirteen children lived; or rather died, for in this same room alone two children had died the day before and one the previous Saturday, as well as an Elizabeth Lush whose death was the subject of an inquest. Altogether ten children had died in the previous six weeks and three more were not expected to live. In the nine years from 1830 to 1838 hundreds of children died at the Cascades factory, and the institution reeled from one scandal to the next. Prostitution, lesbianism and the practice of unnatural sex acts seemed to be rife.

Any woman who became pregnant while in service was sent to the "factory" to have her baby. After the baby was born she had to spend six months in the crime class before being sent out again as a servant. The child, if it survived, would be placed in an orphan school in New Town and mother and child probably never saw one another again. Had Louisa become pregnant during the short time she was with her husband at Crear's? If she had, then there exists no record of a live birth.

This may have been a turning point for Louisa. Her exposure to the "female factory" and the most hardened female convicts in the colony may have left a lasting impression. Her ways were undoubtedly changed and her assignment to the Carter household, where misdemeanours of drunkenness were quashed by her mistress on at least one occasion, led to her ticket-of-leave in 1837. The record shows: 14 March 1837 Ticket-of-Leave/In a public house after hours: reprimanded.

When interviewed by the muster master after arrival, John Jones said he was twenty-eight years old, a tailor by occupation, born at Portallen, County Leitrim, Ireland, and of the Roman Catholic religion. He had brown hair, blue eyes and a dark complexion He stated that he was married to Maria Quinn a "bounty widow" in Devonport, Devon, and could read and write. (A bounty widow was a woman who had received compensation from the government for the death of her husband in the armed forces.)

Jones was given the number *524 Argyle* and assigned to a Mr Lightfoot to work as a tailor. Theophilus Lightfoot had arrived in Hobart on the *Harvey* on 10th July 1827. He established a tailoring business in Elizabeth Street, Hobart Town.

Jones was the first of the grave-robbers to experience imprisonment and hard labour in the colony. In October 1831, following an incident of gross insolence and threatening to take the life of Mr Lightfoot, his master, he was sentenced to six months' imprisonment with hard labour. On his release he was assigned to the interior of the island to work on a road party. In December 1832, under an overseer named Notman, on two occasions eleven days apart, he received twenty-five lashes for neglect of work.

In 1833, to ensure that transportation was an adequate punishment, the authorities in Britain ordered that a due portion of daily labour from each convict should be exacted with no remission or indulgences. This was commented upon by the Reverend John West in his epic "The History of Tasmania": It did not infrequently happen that a tailor or other sedentary craftsman was sentenced to the roads but in breaking stones there is an art and while the dextrous could make every blow effective, the utmost toil of the novice left a deficiency in the task. To admit excuse would have disturbed the calculations of labour and the defaulter was delivered at once to the flogger."

The following year, after giving evidence to the police magistrate, Jones was removed from Notman's road party and sent to the penitentiary, where he worked as a messenger for the colonial gaol. Absenteeism landed him in prison for a further three months before he was assigned to the postmaster in the interior of the island.

In May 1834 he was found prowling around Captain Crear's farm bringing messages to the female servants and making false excuses for his conduct. Was he taking a message from Thomas to Louisa? At the end of that year Jones was found in bed with a female prisoner in his custody and given six months' imprisonment with hard labour.

Jones had again been given the opportunity of practising his trade as a tailor to the road party at Constitution Hill. As usual he abused this privilege, being caught bartering and receiving his fellow convicts' clothing, and sentenced to the road party. He was later caught selling his government-issue books which caused him to be sentenced to the chain-gang at Bridgewater. It was a hard time for Jones and, on completion of his six months, he was assigned to a Mr Brignell. However, by April 1836 he was returned to the government for disorderly conduct and sent to Restdown. It was at this time that, apart from the main road, an assigned party was at Restdown working on the line to the Derwent river. A further assignment to a Mr Simpson saw him again returned to the government in March 1837, with a recommendation that he be returned to the country. Jones' indent records that he was sent to Oatlands for assignment. He finally received his ticket-of-leave that year.

On the deck of the *Argyle* as she lay at anchor in Sullivan's Cove, Richard Thompson gave his age as twenty-four years, and his occupation as a bricklayer's labourer. His place of birth was given as Greenwich, London. He was single, a Roman Catholic, and could read and write. He stated "my reason for saying I was married when taken into custody was because I had a young woman living with me about six or seven months". He had a sister, Bridget, a brother, Shannon, in Wapping, a coal-heaver, and a sister-in-law, Mary Cowburn, in Greenwich. He was given the number *579 Argyle*.

Richard Thompson's trade as a bricklayer's labourer landed him with an assignment to the government stone-mason, John Addison, Superintendent of Government Masons. It was gross insubordination to Mr Addison that led, on 20 August 1835, to his sentence being extended by a year.

Thompson spent most of his eight years between the prisoners' barracks and his assignments associated with stone-masonry. Like Goslin and Jones, Thompson was indifferent to his situation, and to ease his pain he drank, was insolent, lazy, and absented himself on various occasions. He once received thirty-six lashes for being "absent from his gang about 2 o'clock". In September 1832 for the offence of drunkenness he was sent to the treadwheel for ten days; he later served seven days on the treadwheel; and six Saturday afternoons had to be spent there. Another offence of drunkenness brought him six days solitary confinement on bread and water. He was not free until 1838.

When convicts had served their sentences they faced the problem of earning a living. The stigma of having been a convict attached to them and if they were unskilled and illiterate this added to their difficulties. In spite of this there were opportunities for a good, new life and some convicts managed to succeed. Ex-convicts who did not manage to make a new life for themselves often ended their days in lunatic asylums or as imperial paupers supported by the government of the day.

Tickets-of-leave required the convicts to live and work in the area in the jurisdiction of the magistrate who granted the ticket. Conditional pardons were given for hard work or good conduct; the convict was technically free but required to stay in the colony, rather than just a district, for the remainder of the sentence imposed in Britain. An absolute pardon, cancelling the remainder of the sentence, could only be granted by the Crown on the recommendation of the Lieutenant Governor. An absolute pardon meant a convict was free to leave the colony if they wished.

Thomas Goslin and his accomplices could read and write and three of them had some skills. Had they been capable of ceasing their criminal behaviour or had they wanted to reform, they would have taken advantage of the reward system so carefully explained to them by the Lieutenant Governor when they arrived in Van Diemen's Land. Had they conformed they would have escaped the harsh punishments they brought upon themselves. Yet the catalogue of offences committed by the men showed a total indifference to improving their lot. It seems unlikely therefore that when they received their tickets-of-leave they would have become law-abiding citizens overnight.

On 11 June 1838 John Jones requested permission to marry Jane Thomas, a free settler, and the marriage is recorded on his indent.

Thereafter no trace has been found of any of the gang. Their names were relatively common among the convicts and free settlers of Van Diemen's Land in the 1840s and not all records have survived. There was, in fact, another John Jones transported in the *Argyle* in 1831 and the convict records sometimes confuse the two, although the grave-robbing John Jones was a tailor while the other was a millwright. Among convict societies aliases were in common use and, as they used aliases throughout their criminal careers, this gang may have used new names to begin their new lives but, not knowing if they did or what those aliases might have been, it has so far proved impossible to trace them after 1840.

In his "Life of Sir Astley Cooper" published in 1843, Bransby Cooper commented that "Vaughan and his wife have never returned to this country although the period of their banishment has long expired".

CHAPTER SEVENTEEN

The Italian Boy

While Thomas and Louisa Vaughan (aka Goslin), Richard Thompson and John Jones were beginning their servitude in Van Diemen's Land, events took place in London which were to have a significant effect on the bodysnatchers' trade.

On 5 November 1831 John Bishop, a man with a long history of stealing bodies, took the body of a teenage boy to King's College Hospital, London, in the hope of selling it to the anatomy department. William Hill, the dissecting room porter at King's College Hospital, was struck by the freshness of the corpse. Hill said he had to ask Richard Partridge, the anatomist, whether he wished to buy the body and Hill took the opportunity to tell Partridge of his concerns about the corpse. Partridge immediately saw that blood was oozing from the gums as well as from a cut on the dead boy's forehead. He told Hill to offer nine guineas for the corpse. After consulting with James May, a confederate who accompanied him, Bishop reluctantly accepted the nine guineas although they had been hoping for ten guineas.

Partridge asked Bishop and May to wait while he changed a £50 note so that he could pay them. This was a ploy to give Partridge time to call the police and for them to arrive.

The police arrested John Bishop, 33, James May, 30, and a member of the gang waiting outside, Thomas Williams, 28, on suspicion of murder.

On Sunday 6 November an autopsy was carried out by a surgeon, Mr George Beaman, who found that the body not only had never been buried but it had never even been prepared for burial. He found a small wound on the boy's forehead, his teeth were missing and his gums oozed blood. Not long before death the boy had had meal of potatoes and rum. Mr Beaman concluded death had been caused by a blow to the back of the head.

The identity of the corpse was unknown and when the dead lad remained unidentified a consensus grew that it was one of the boys brought from Italy by older Italian men and put to work as beggars in London. The boys' good looks made them sympathetic figures successful at attracting alms. It came to be believed that the dead boy was Carlo Ferrari, a young Italian beggar known to have carried a cage containing white mice which he displayed when he was given a coin.

A Coroner's Inquest was held and the jury heard that May had used a bradawl to gouge out the dead boy's teeth hoping to sell them for twenty-one shillings. The dentist who bought them, Thomas Mills, gave evidence that May had offered him twelve teeth which still had bits of gum attached to them. He claimed May had told him the teeth came from the body of a boy aged between fourteen and fifteen years of age who had never been buried. Mills paid twelve shillings for them not the twenty-one shillings May had asked because one chipped tooth lowered the value. On 10 November 1831 the jury returned a verdict of wilful murder against some person or persons unknown and they urged the police to investigate the involvement of Bishop and Williams.

John Bishop had married his father's widow, Sarah. She had been the elder Bishop's third wife. John and Sarah lived at number 3 Nova Scotia Gardens, Bethnal Green, London, with their three children and Thomas Williams and his wife Rhoda who was Bishop's seventeen year old step daughter/half sister. A search of Bishop's home produced grave-robbing equipment. The house had a garden with a privy at the end and a well in the centre. Buried in the garden were items of boys' clothing; a woman's shawl was recovered from the well while at the bottom of the privy the police found a scalp with long hair attached. When Thomas Williams, who had been born Thomas Head, moved to Nova Scotia

Gardens he rented number 2 but when he married Rhoda he moved into number 3 with Bishop and his family and joined Bishop in his body-snatching activities. In spite of the fact that Williams had not lived at number 2 for many weeks and the house was occupied by another family, the police searched number 2 and from the privy at the bottom of that garden they retrieved a bundle of women's clothes.

The news of the murder of the Italian Boy, as he became called, spread great alarm among Londoners and revived memories of the Burke and Hare murders in Edinburgh three years earlier. Families who had lost touch with relatives made strenuous efforts to find their lost ones or to lay the disappearance at John Bishop's door. The sisters of Fanny Pighorn, a single mother who earned her living as a washerwoman, had become concerned because Fanny had suddenly disappeared. When they inspected the clothing found at Nova Scotia Gardens they identified it as having belonged to Fanny. The police were able to find records at a private anatomy school of a body matching Fanny's description having been sold to it by John Bishop. They also found witnesses who had seen Fanny in the company of Bishop and Williams shortly before she disappeared.

At a hearing at Bow Street Magistrates' Court opened on 18th November Bishop, Williams and May appeared charged with the murder of the Italian Boy. The prosecution presented the findings of the Coroner's Inquest, the evidence the police had gathered and statements from witnesses. Bishop, Williams and May were committed to Newgate Prison to await their trial at the Old Bailey in December for the murder of Carlo Ferrari. In case a new or positive identity of the murdered boy was made or the boy turned out not to be Carlo Ferrari a second charge was brought of wilful murder of a person unknown.

On Friday 2 December the trial at the Old Bailey opened. It had been expected that Bishop and Williams would be charged with three counts: the murder of Carlo Ferrari or unknown boy, of Fanny Pighorn, and of an unknown person whose clothes had been found buried in Bishop's garden. May was expected to face only one charge. In the event the prosecution did not proceed with the charge of murder in the case of Fanny Pighorn because her body was not available to substantiate the charge. Instead Bishop, Williams and May were charged only with the murder of Carlo Ferrari and/or "a male person whose name is unknown".

The trial was conducted before three judges and a jury. The prisoners all pleaded "Not Guilty". The prosecution called many witnesses who built up a circumstantial but compelling case against Bishop and Williams. The Court heard statements from Bishop saying that he dealt only with bodies that had died a natural death and that Williams and May had no knowledge of how he had obtained the boy's body. Williams' statement claimed he had no knowledge of how Bishop came to have the body; he said he had simply gone along with the transaction without asking questions and had broken no laws. May's statement said he had trafficked in anatomical subjects for six years but never resorted to murder to obtain a body and he had no idea how Bishop procured the dead boy. The Italian Boy was believed to have been murdered on the night of 3 November. A witness gave evidence that May had spent that night with her in her home. As May was a married man and the witness was a single woman admitting to adultery little weight was given to the testimony.

The Lord Chief Justice summed up the evidence for the jury which deliberated for thirty minutes before returning "Guilty" verdicts against all three. The sentences of "death by hanging" were passed with the order that the bodies were to be given to the anatomists for dissection. The executions were to take place on the Monday.

The prisoners were taken back to Newgate and lodged in the condemned cells. Each was offered the comfort of a clergyman.

Many of those present at the trial had expected that May would be found "Not Guilty". In his condemned cell Bishop wrote his confession and again insisted May was innocent of murder. He urged the authorities to get May's verdict overturned. Williams too in the confession he made stated that May was innocent. May himself, when asked if he wished to make a confession, said he had been guilty of many offences in his life but had never committed murder.

There was no Court of Appeal in those days. The only way a sentence could be altered was by making an appeal to the Home Secretary and hoping he would intervene. On the Saturday evening the confessions made by Bishop, Williams and May were taken to the Lord Chief Justice to see if there were grounds for asking the Home Secretary to intervene in May's case.

On Sunday, with May still protesting his innocence and Bishop and Williams telling anyone who would listen that May was innocent, the clergymen counselling the prisoners called a further meeting of the judges. They then sent a request to the Home Secretary, together with copies of Bishop and Williams' confessions, for the verdict to be reconsidered. As soon as it was received the Home Secretary's decision was relayed to the prisoners. Bishop and Williams were to hang but May was not to suffer death. On hearing the news May quite literally had a fit.

His sentence was reduced to imprisonment with transportation to Botany Bay for life. He was sent to a prison hulk but later transferred to a hospital ship where he died. No cause of death was given.

While the prisoners slept a scaffold with three nooses was put up outside the prison and a crowd estimated at between 30,000 and 40,000 gathered. When daylight

Newgate prison.

came the third noose was removed and the crowd realised that May was not to hang. At eight o'clock when Bishop calmly walked on to the scaffold there was a roar from the crowd. Williams was very nervous and agitated. Hoods were placed over their heads and a noose placed around each neck. While they were saying their last prayers a silent signal was given to the hangman to make the drop. Bishop died instantly but Williams slowly strangled to death. At nine o'clock the bodies were put into a cart and taken to be ceremonially cut open and sewn up again. Bishop was removed to King's College Hospital where Richard Partridge opened and examined the body before sewing it up again so that it could be exhibited to the crowd anxious to see Bishop. Later students and lecturers dissected the body until nothing remained. Williams' body was given to a private medical school and paying visitors were allowed to watch it being dissected.

Bishop's confession, in accordance with custom, was published. It had taken care to exonerate all members of his family. Bishop began by declaring and confessing that the boy supposed to be a Italian boy was in fact a Lincolnshire drover's boy who he and Williams had plied with drink at various public houses before taking him home. While his family slept Bishop fed the boy bread and cheese and gave him a glass of rum mixed with laudanum. When the boy was asleep they tied a rope around his feet, took him into the garden and Bishop put him head first into the well until he was almost totally immersed while Williams held the rope to make sure the body did not get out of their control. When they were sure the boy was dead, they recovered the body, stripped it and buried the clothes in the garden. They put the body in the wash house and went out for a coffee. When they returned they doubled the body over and put it into a box which they fastened with ropes to prevent anyone opening it. They then went to bed.

Bishop gave a detailed account of how they met a woman who said she was homeless. He and Williams spent the day drinking with her before taking her to their home and slipping laudanum in her drink.

When she too slept she was taken out and put in the well. She struggled so they tied the end of the rope to a gatepost and went for a walk while she died. When they returned they stripped the body and put the bundled up clothes down the privy of the then unoccupied 2 Nova Scotia Gardens. Again the body was doubled up, put into a box and taken to a private medical school where they were paid eight guineas for it. Bishop said it was not until later that he learned the victim's name was Fanny Pighorn.

Bishop also confessed to killing a boy of ten or eleven years of age in the same way as the others and selling his body to St Bartholomew's Hospital for eight guineas.

Bishop went on to say that in the course of a twelve year career he had obtained and sold between 500 and 1,000 bodies but never resorted to murder except in the cases he confessed to.

Thomas Willliams' confession agreed that all Bishop had said was the truth. That he had not been involved in any other murders nor had he ever sold any body except the ones he was involved in with Bishop. He added that May was wholly innocent and ignorant of the murders.

CHAPTER EIGHTEEN

The Demise of Grave-Robbing

While the authorities had been happy to turn a blind-eye to the complicity of the medical profession with grave-robbing, public concern and anger against the practice had been mounting. As Thomas Vaughan (aka Goslin) found on a number of occasions, once he had been arrested for taking bodies from their graves, he was at risk of injury, perhaps even death, from the large and furious crowds that gathered in the hope of taking their anger out on him. Dr Knox felt the full fury of the inhabitants of Edinburgh after the Burke and Hare murders came to light.

Thomas Wakely, who was a surgeon, coroner, medical reformer, first editor of the *Lancet*, and Member of Parliament for Finsbury, had long been campaigning against nepotism and practices at the Royal College of Surgeons and the medical profession in general. Public anger against graverobbing forced Parliament to set up a Select Committee, chaired by Wakely, to enquire into the manner of obtaining subjects for dissection in the schools of anatomy and into the state of the law affecting persons employed in obtaining or dissecting bodies.

Surgeons, doctors, policemen and bodysnatchers were among those who appeared before the Inquiry. Sir Astley Cooper gave evidence of the rise in the prices paid for corpses during the time he had practised surgery. Asked what sort of men were engaged in stealing corpses he described them as "the lowest dregs of degradation" but he praised their efficiency, saying they would be able to obtain for him the body of anyone he wanted. J.G. Glennon, a London policeman, told the Select Committee of the practices used to acquire corpses and said he had been responsible for recovering fifty bodies taken through burglary of private houses. Mr James Somerville, MD, when asked, "What is your opinion as to the possibility of obtaining a supply of bodies by sale or bequest?" answered "that such a supply would be found amongst the lowest order of Irish who, I believe, conceive that their duties to the dead are discharged when the wake is over".

The main recommendation of the Select Committee was that as there was a need for the study of anatomy by dissection, the best way of supplying the bodies was by using the bodies of the poor whose corpse was not claimed by relatives or friends for burial.

In 1829 an Act was drawn up to regulate the supply of bodies to anatomy schools. It was passed by the House of Commons but rejected by the House of Lords.

Public anger, alarm and revulsion following the Bishop and Williams murders made the authorities realise that something had to be done and quickly. Dealing with the supply of bodies for medical schools became an urgent problem. Following swiftly on the execution of Bishop and Williams, the second Anatomy Bill was introduced in the House of Commons and soon after had its second reading. Although there was still some opposition, it was passed in the House of Commons and in the House of Lords and in summer 1832 became law. The bodies of paupers, unclaimed by family or friends, who died in workhouses or hospitals could legally be dissected by surgeons to teach anatomy. There have been very few alterations to the Anatomy Act of 1832 from that day to this.

At the same time as the new Act became law, the earlier Act ordering that the bodies of hanged murderers should be given to surgeons for dissection was repealed.

It took time to set up the bureaucracy and bring the Act into effect so graverobbing did not cease immediately. The Act called for an Inspector of Anatomy to be appointed to oversee the distribution of bodies to the schools. The implementation of the Act saw hospitals competing for bodies; some even bribed officials. Some hospitals offered preferential treatment for the poor of parishes that co-operated in supplying that hospital with their dead. Some parishes, however, withheld their dead for fear of public reaction.

The poor, with justification, believed that they were discriminated against in that their dead were the most likely to end up in the anatomy schools since the supply was obtained mainly from workhouses, hospitals, prisons, asylums and hulks. The Act forced poor people to provide for their own burial or face the consequences. There was provision for paupers to leave instructions with a workhouse that they did not wish to be dissected after death but there was a danger that their instructions might not be acted upon. The fear of ending up in an anatomy school was so great that the custom of insuring for a "decent burial" became so widespread among the poor that they were said to be more interested in death insurance than life insurance. This was the motivation behind the growth of the poor setting aside a tiny sum each week to ensure that, because they could pay for their own burial, their dead bodies were not sent to the anatomy schools by the parish. Fear of being forced by circumstances to enter a workhouse, with the likelihood of eventually being delivered to the anatomy schools, was so great that people would go to great lengths to avoid it. Many preferred to starve, emigrate, turn to prostitution or commit suicide rather than go into a workhouse.

The Act gradually regularised the supply of bodies to hospitals and led to the demise of the private anatomy schools, so that by the end of the nineteenth century there were none.

While the bureaucracy and implementation of the Act were put into working order, graverobbing supplied the shortfall but ten years after the Act was passed into law bodysnatching ceased to be a highly-paid, low-risk job and petered out.